Items should be returned to the library from which they were borrowed on or before the date stamped above, unless a renewal has been granted.

Old Mother

A Wild West Pantomime Adventure

Paul Reakes

Samuel French — London
New York - Toronto - Hollywood

CHARACTERS

Old Mother Hubbard
Hughie, her son
Polly, her daughter
Dandy, her dog
First Bailiff
Second Bailiff
The Good Fairy
Tex Laramie
Old Tumbleweed
Matt Vinyl
Hank
Jake
Miss Lulabelle
Little Deer, a Red Indian Maiden
Chief Thunder Cloud, her father
Little Drizzle, his son
A Grizzly Bear
The Medicine Man
Major Day
Chorus of villagers, children, cowboys, cowgirls, townsfolk, Red
Indians, cavalry

SYNOPSIS OF SCENES

ACT I

ACT II

MUSIC PLOT

ACT I

1.	Song and Dance	Chorus, Children and Dancers
2.	Song and Dance	Hughie, Dandy and Children
3.	Comedy Song and Dance	Mother Hubbard and Dancers
Reprise of No. 3		All
4.	Sing-a-Long	Hughie, Polly, Dandy and Children from the audience
5.	Song	Children
6.	Song	Tex and Chorus
7.	Song and Dance	Chorus and Dancers
8.	Comedy Trio and Dance	Vinyl, Hank and Jake
9.	Song and Dance	Mother Hubbard, Tex, Polly, Hughie, Dandy, Tumbleweed and Chorus
Reprise of No. 9		All

ACT II

10.	Song	Tumbleweed and Chorus
10a.	Dance	Lulabelle and Dancers
11.	Song and Dance	Hughie, Little Deer and Chorus
12.	Comedy Dance	Lulabelle and Dancers
13.	Duet	Tex and Polly
14.	Comedy Duet	Mother Hubbard and Tumbleweed
15.	Song	Chorus
16.	Dance	Dancers or Solo Dancer
17.	Song and Dance	All
18.	Sing-a-Long	Mother, Hughie, Dandy and the audience
19.	Final Song	All

CHARACTERS

Old Mother Hubbard (Dame) is a lovable, energetic old girl who enjoys both fun and misery and never misses an opportunity of involving the audience. All her costumes should be outrageous and funny. She wears her "poor" costume with lots of comic patches and darns etc., a couple of very ludicrous cowgirl outfits, and a loud gingham dress with apron etc. Outrageous Red Indian Squaw Finale costume.

Hughie is her son, a likeable young buffoon. He provides plenty of comic antics and audience participation. A good singing voice and dancing ability an advantage. Comic "poor" costume and ridiculous cowboy outfit with huge stetson and enormous fur chaps etc. Finale costume.

Polly is her pretty, young daughter. Charming of manner and sweet of voice, but never soppy or simpering. "Poor", but picturesque costume, and very becoming cowgirl outfits. Finale costume.

Dandy is indeed a wonder dog. He can dance, howl in tune, understand human conversations, communicate with bears, and rescue everyone just in the nick of time. In fact, he is so wonderful, you might be tempted into thinking that he is really a human being in a dog's skin!

The Bailiffs are a slapstick duo. First Bailiff is a rather pompous little man, while Second Bailiff is just a big, gullible nitwit. Matching comic official outfits. They only appear in Act I.

The Good Fairy first appears as a frail, old beggar woman in a tattered hooded cloak. Then, in a flash and a puff of smoke, she is revealed in all her shining, magical magnificence. A graceful presence and pleasant speaking voice is essential. Finale costume. She only appears in Act I and Finale Act II.

Tex Laramie (Principal boy) is a tall, dashing young cowboy with a wide smile, a forthright manner and the best legs in the West! A strong singing voice and a well-sustained "Western" accent is essential. He wears a white stetson, a fringed suede jacket, skin-tight blue jeans and cowboy boots. Gun with holster. Finale costume.

Old Tumbleweed is a bewhiskered, dust-covered, disreputable, but very lovable old son-of-a-gun in the best "Gabby Hayes" tradition. A good "Western" drawl is essential. He takes a great fancy to Mother Hubbard and never misses an opportunity of wooing her in true pioneer fashion. Battered old hat, red flannel "granddad" vest, shapeless trousers or jeans and boots. Old gun with shabby holster.

Matt Vinyl is the meanest varmint ever to grace a wanted poster! The badman's baddie — the one we all love to hate. "Western" accent essential. Black hat, dark period (Victorian) suit with fancy waistcoat and boots. Fancy gun and holster.

Hank and **Jake** are Vinyl's bully boys — all brawn and no brain. Rough "Western" accents with outfits to match. Guns with holsters.

Miss Lulabelle, the dancer, is the main attraction at the Silver Dollar Saloon. Good acting and dancing ability is essential. She is a slinky, seductive siren with everything in the right place ! A dancing version of Mae West. Flamboyant saloon dancer's costume.

Little Deer is your typical Red Indian beauty. Her broken English is charming and her movements are swift and agile. Black, plaited hair with headband and feather, short Red Indian dress revealing plenty of tanned leg, necklace and moccasins. Finale costume. She only appears in Act II.

Chief Thunder Cloud is a tall, imposing person, with a deep rich voice and a very dignified manner. He only loses his decorum when dealing with his irritating children — especially Little Drizzle! Magnificent Red Indian Chief's costume with large feathered head-dress. He only appears in Act II.

Little Drizzle (child's part) tries to be a miniature copy of his illustrious dad — with comic results! Small version of Chief's costume with small feathered head-dress. He only appears in Act II.

The Grizzly Bear is a mountain of furry ferociousness towards the baddies, but charm itself towards the goodies. A good bear's skin. It only appears in Act II.

The Medicine Man is really Oswald, the long lost brother of Mother Hubbard (this should not be revealed in the programme). At the hands of villainous Vinyl, he received a knock on the head and suffered from amnesia. Befriended by the Indians, he becomes their industrious and frightening Medicine Man, complete with wild yelps and strange little dances. After a second knock on the head, his memory and true nature return, showing him to be a mild-mannered and amiable little chap. Red Indian Medicine Man's costume with mask and head-dress with horns, etc. He only appears in Act II.

Major Day is a fine specimen of the US Cavalry. An authoritative figure with a commanding voice. US Cavalry officer's uniform, with sword etc. He only appears in Act II.

The Chorus, Dancers and Children have lots to do, appearing as snooty villagers, village children, cowboys, cowgirls, townsfolk of Deadman's Gulch, Red Indian braves, the Red Indian tribe, scalping ceremony dancers and the US Cavalry. All participate in the action and musical numbers.

PRODUCTION NOTES

Staging
The pantomime offers opportunities for elaborate staging, but can be produced quite simply if facilities and funds are limited. There are four full sets: Outside Old Mother Hubbard's Cottage, The Town of Deadman's Gulch, The Silver Dollar Saloon, The Red Indian camp (this can be used for the Finale). There are two half sets: Old Mother Hubbard's Cottage, The Log Cabin in the Hills. These scenes are interlinked with tabs or frontcloth scenes. If there is only space enough to hang one frontcloth, please use it for the "Prairie" scenes. The "Village Street" can be played to tabs.

Mother Hubbard's Cupboard
It is backless and set against an escape opening in the back wall flat of the cottage interior. This opening is concealed by a black curtain.

Gun Shots
This effect is optional but how can you have a "Wild West" setting without a few shots being fired? However, special care must be paid to the firing of blanks on stage and the advice of the appropriate authorities should be sought. And a note in the programme, stating that guns are fired during a performance, is strongly advisable.

The Swing Doors
These are a must. No respectable saloon would be without them. First seen from the outside in Act I, Scene 5, they can be easily utilized and seen from the inside in Act II, Scene 1. It is advisable to have them well in use before the actual performance to ensure a slick routine.

Western Accents
It goes without saying that these must be well sustained by all actors playing "Wild West" roles. We have all seen enough "Cowboy an' Injuns" films to make them part of our language.

Other pantomimes by Paul Reakes published by Samuel French Ltd

Babes in the Wood
Bang You're Dead!
Little Jack Horner
Little Miss Muffet: a Pantomime
Mantrap
Santa in Space: a Christmas Pantomime Adventure
Sinbad the Sailor

ACT I

Prominent up R *is Old Mother Hubbard's shabby, tumbledown cottage. Neat cottages and trees on* L. *Village backcloth and ground row*

When the CURTAIN *rises the villagers, their children and the dancers are discovered. They go straight into the opening song and dance*

Song 1

After the song, the dancers exit

The adult villagers look at Old Mother Hubbard's cottage with disgust

First Man Just look at the state of Old Mother Hubbard's cottage!
Villagers Disgusting!
First Woman (*a real sourpuss*) We'll never win the best kept village competition with that eyesore on display!
First Man No! (*Local village*) will beat us hollow!
Second Woman I heard —

The others gather around, eager for gossip

I heard she hasn't paid her rent for months!

They react

And — the squire is sending his bailiffs here today to evict her!

First Woman And a good thing too! I shall be glad to see the back of Mother Hubbard and her family.

First Man Aye! And Dandy! That noisy dog of theirs!

Children (*protesting and forming a separate group*) We like Dandy!!

Villagers (*aghast*) What!

First Girl Mother Hubbard is a nice, friendly old lady!

First Boy Unlike some we could mention!

The children eye the First Woman accusingly

First Woman Well, really! (*To the audience*) In my opinion, all children should be seen and not heard!

The villagers scold the children

Loud barking is heard, and Dandy the dog bounds on. With great delight, the children gather round him

Children (*patting and making a great fuss of him*) Dandy! Hallo, Dandy! Nice boy! *etc., etc.*

Dandy rolls over and lets them tickle his belly

Hughie (*off* L) Dandy! Here, boy! (*He whistles*)

Hughie Hubbard enters from L

Dandy bounds over to him. Hughie shakes his paw

Hughie (*greeting the audience*) Hallo folks! Hi kids! (*He waves*) I'm Hughie Hubbard and this is Dandy, the wonder dog! Wave to the nice people, Dandy!

Dandy waves

He's clever, isn't he? He makes Lassie look like Pluto! Now, if you all shout "Hallo Dandy", he'll answer you! Yes, he will! Come on, after three! One - two - three!

Audience Hallo, Dandy!

Dandy (*to the audience*) Woof! Woof!

Hughie See! That was doggerel, that was. He said "Hallo, ladies and gentlemen and boys and girls. What a great pleasure it is to make your acquaintance!" (*To Dandy*) That's what you said, didn't you?

Dandy (*nodding*) Woof!

Hughie (*to the audience*) I suppose you've heard all about our troubles from old Dot Cotton (*or other TV busybody*) over there! (*He indicates the First Woman*)

Dandy growls in her direction

(*To the audience*) Yes, we're broke! Skint! We're all trying to raise some money to pay the rent. Poor old Mum and sister Polly are out now selling firewood! Dandy and me have been doin' a bit of buskin'. Without success, eh, Dandy?

Dandy gives a dismal howl and covers his eyes with his paws

It was a complete waste of time!

Dandy nudges him and points to the villagers

No, they won't give us anything!

Dandy demonstrates "have a go"

All right, but it'll be a waste of time! (*They go up to the villagers in a . showbiz manner*) Ladles and jellyspoons, your attention perlease! Pin back yer lugoles, and listen to Hughie and Dandy!

They strike poses

Your very own - (*the latest on the pop scene*)!!

Song 2

Hughie sings and Dandy accompanies him with howls. They perform a comic dance as the children take up the song. After the song, the children clap and cheer. The adults are unimpressed. Hughie goes round with his hat out. Dandy sits up and begs. The children are about to give him some money, but the adults pull them away. Hughie and Dandy move away, very downcast

Hughie (*to Dandy*) I told you it'd be a a a waste of time, old son! (*To the audience, pointing to villagers*) That lot are so tight, they could peel oranges in their pockets!

Old Mother Hubbard and Polly enter at the back of the auditorium. Both carry baskets containing bundles of firewood

Mother (*calling out*) Yoo hoo!
Hughie Here comes Mum, Dandy! Hallo Mum! (*He waves*)

Dandy barks and waves his paw

Mother Firewood! Firewood for sale! Get yer loverly firewood 'ere! *Etc., etc!*

Comic business and by-play as Mother and Polly make their way through the audience to the stage

(*Mounting the stage and waving cheerfully to the villagers*) 'Ello, neighbours!
Polly Hallo, everybody!

The villagers coldly turn their backs and stick their noses in the air

Mother (*to the audience*) Crikey! We're about as popular as the Council Tax! (*or topical gag*)

The children come forward and greet Mother and Polly warmly

Children Hallo, Mother Hubbard! Hallo, Polly!
Mother 'Ello, me dears! Well, it's nice to see the 'Ubbard family 'ave still got some friends! (*She nods at the villagers*) What's up with the "New Kids on the Block" over there? They look as if someone's frozen their assets!
Polly I expect they've heard about our insolvency.

Mother Yes. (*Double take*) Our what?!

Polly They know we're broke!

Mother Why didn't you say that in the first place! These foreign languages! (*To the audience*) That's what comes of sendin' 'em to (*local school*).

Dandy bounds over and makes a great fuss of her

Hallo, Dandy! Ahh! Who loves 'is Mummy den?

Dandy licks her

Oy! Careful! Don't lick all the paint off! It took me four hours an' two trowels to put this lot on! (*To the audience*) 'E loves my new perfume! It's Kennel No. Nine!

Polly Did you have any luck with your busking, Hughie?

Hughie sadly shows the insides of his empty pockets. Dandy howls dismally

Hughie Did you two sell any firewood?

Mother (*showing basket*) Not a flippin' twig! We tried everywhere, even (*local posh area*)!

Polly Mum, let's try selling some to the people here (*She indicates the villagers*)

Hughie Ha! You won't get a penny out of that lot!

Mother You just leave 'em to me! I could sell snow to Eskimos! (*or local/ topical gag. She moves to one of the male villagers*) How about you, Rambo? You look like you could use something to get your fire going!!

The man's wife pulls him away

(*To First Man*) Firewood, sir? Only a shilling a bundle!

The man takes a bundle and scrutinizes it very closely

(*To the audience*) 'E thinks 'e's on the Antiques Roadshow!

First Man (*throwing the bundle back*) Pah! There's not much there for a shilling!

Mother Ah! But it's of the finest quality. I 'ad to smash up my poor old Granny's antique toilet seat get to get that! Granny was heartbroken - she was sittin' on it at the time! It won't take much to light it. It's still warm! (*She holds out bundle*) Feel!

The man turns away

(*To First Woman*) Would modom care to puchase some firewood?
First Woman Certainly not! Go away!
Mother Just think, you could glue all the bits together an' make yerself a new broomstick!

She and the children hoot with laughter

Oh, come on, be good neighbours an' 'elp us out! If we don't get some dosh from somewhere, we'll be kicked out!
Villagers And good riddance!
First Woman The sooner you're thrown out of this village the better!
Villagers Hear, hear!!

Growling and barking, Dandy bounds at the villagers and chases them out in all directions

The First Woman is the last to go. Dandy pounces on the end of her skirt. It rips and falls down, revealing long, comic bloomers. The others roar with laughter

The woman gathers up her skirt and tries to make a dignified exit. The children follow her off, jeering and laughing

Mother (*melodramatically*) Oh! Misery me! What's to become of us? No money to pay the rent! Cast out! It's the cold, wet streets from now on!

Hughie and Sally put comforting arms around her

Hughie Cheer up, Mum. We've still got each other.
Polly Yes, we're still a family.
Dandy (*nestling up to Mother*) Woof!
Mother If only my brother Ossie were 'ere! He'd 'elp us out. He wouldn't

let his little sister suffer this humidifyin' situation!
Polly But Uncle Ossie's abroad somewhere. We haven't seen or heard
from him for years.

*Mother gives a deep sigh and extracts a large, gaudy handkerchief from
her knicker leg. She blows hard*

Come on, Hughie, let's try selling some firewood at the other end of the
village. You can come as well, Dandy.

Polly and Hughie exit L *with baskets. Dandy follows, gives Mother a sad
wave, then exits*

Mother (*to the audience*) Oh, that this should 'appen to 'em. It's not fair,
is it? Oh, come on! Don't take a vote on it. I said, (*shouting*) it's not fair,
is it?

The audience shouts back

I've always managed to pay me way up till now! (*Big sigh*) Still, I
mustn't let it get me down. Always try to look on the bright side, that's
my motto!

Song 3

*After the song, the dancers enter and sweep Mother along in an
energetic dance*

*Comic business with her being thrown about and trying to copy the dance
steps with disastrous results*

It ends with her crawling, on all fours, into her cottage

The children rush on from R

First Boy Where's Old Mother Hubbard?
Dancer Gone inside to look for some "Sanatogen".

The dancers exit L *laughing*

First Girl We've got to do something! The bailiffs will be here any minute to throw her out of her cottage!

First Boy (*looking off* R) Here they come now!

First Girl Come on! Let's go and warn her!

The children exit quickly into the cottage

To suitable music, the Bailiffs enter from R *doing their comic march*

They parade around until the Second Bailiff catches sight of the audience. He comes to an abrupt halt, causing the First Bailiff to crash into him. They both fall over. Cut music. Comic business as they try to get up, but find that their legs have become entangled. Finally, they sort themselves out and stand up

First Bailiff Why did you do that, you twit!

Second Bailiff (*dumbly*) Wot?

First Bailiff Stop without giving a signal?!

Second Bailiff I seen somefink!

First Bailiff No, no, no! (*He corrects him*) I saw something! I saw something!

Second Bailiff Oh, you did as well!

First Bailiff No, you nitwit! I was correcting your speech! Your grammar is shocking sometimes!

Second Bailiff I know! She's not been the same since she joined the (*local OAP's club*)!

First Bailiff Not your grandma! I meant ... Oh, never mind! What was it you seen ...er... saw?

Second Bailiff whispers in his ear and points towards the audience. Both peer out

Oo! It's people!

Second Bailiff (*nervously*) T ... T ... there's a lot of them! (*He whispers*) Are they asleep?

First Bailiff (*whispering back*) I'll find out. (*He yells at the audience*) Are you asleep?!!

The audience yell back. Second Bailiff leaps into First Bailiff's arms

First Bailiff Get off! Get off! (*He lets him drop to the ground*) What's the matter with you?! (*He hauls him up*)

Second Bailiff (*gaping at the audience in terror*) I... I'm s... s... scared! (*He buries his face in the First Bailiff's coat*)

First Bailiff (*pushing him away*) Stop doing that! There's nothing to be scared of. They're perfectly harmless. (*He shouts at the audience*) Aren't you?!!

The audience shout back. The Second Bailiff jumps back and starts trembling with fear

First Bailiff If the Squire saw you carrying on like that, he'd give you the sack! Bailiffs are supposed to be tough! (*He takes out an eviction order*) Come on, we've got to slap this eviction order on Old Mother Hubbard! Let's get on with it!

He drags him up to the cottage

> *The children come out carrying a large sign. It reads "Danger! Infectious Disease! Keep out!" They hang it on the door*

First Bailiff Hey! What's this?!

First Boy Can't you read?

First Bailiff Infectious diseases! Who's infected?

First Girl Old Mother Hubbard! She's got the dreaded lurgi and it's highly contagious!

Second Bailiff (*repulsed*) Ugh!! Let's get away from here! (*He makes for exit*)

First Bailiff (*pulling him back*) Wait a minute! (*To First Girl*) Highly contagious, eh? Then how come you lot were in there?

First Boy (*jumping in quick*) It only affects grown ups! Even Doctor (*local*)won't come near the place!

First Bailiff Pull the other one! This is just a put up job to stop us evicting Old Mother Hubbard! I'm going in!

He makes for the door, but the children close ranks in front of it

First Girl I wouldn't if I were you! (*To Second Bailiff*) Do you know what happens if you catch the dreaded lurgi?
Second Bailiff N... No!
First Boy It's horrible!

All the children groan and make horrible faces

First Girl First you feel very, very hot!

Business as Second Bailiff pants and fans himself

First Boy Then you feel very, very cold!

Business as he shivers and his teeth chatter

First Girl Then you start to itch all over!

Business as he scratches uncontrollably

First Boy Then you turn yellow!

Business as he examines himself

Second Bailiff (*to the audience, in a panic*) Am I turnin' yellow?!!
Children (*encouraging the audience*) Yes!
Second Bailiff (*beside himself*) Ahh! I've got it! I've got the dreaded lurgi!! Help!!

He runs out R screaming

First Bailiff Ha! You might have frightened him off, but you don't scare me! (*He makes for the cottage door*) Out of my way!
First Boy You haven't heard the worse part yet! As soon as you've finished boilin', freezin', itchin' and turnin' yellow — all your hair falls out!
First Girl And you shrink! Every bit of you — except your head! And that swells up to four times its normal size!
First Bailiff Ha! What a load of rubbish! Let me get to that door! (*He pushs the children aside and hammers on the door*) Come on, Mother

Hubbard! Open up!! (*To the audience, turning his back on the door*)
Turning yellow! Shrinking! Heads swelling up! They must think I'm a
right wally to believe that rubbish!

*While his back is turned, the cottage door opens and a very small Mother
Hubbard appears. It is in fact a little girl, wearing an exact replica of
Mother Hubbard's costume and hat. She also wears an enormous
yellow dummy head, that looks as much like Mother Hubbard as
possible*

Little Girl Hallo! Can I help you?
First Bailiff About time... (*He turns*) Are you...? (*He just gapes in mute
terror*)
Little Girl (*advancing on him*) I'm Old Mother Hubbard.

The First Bailiff screams, and runs out R

The children roar with laughter

First Boy (*calling into the cottage*) All clear! They've gone!

The real Mother Hubbard comes out of the cottage and cheers

*She removes the dummy head from the little girl and shakes her hand. The
music starts and they all go into a short reprise of Song 3. The Lights fade
to Black-out*

SCENE 2

Village Street. Tabs, or a front cloth showing the outskirts of the village

Hughie and Polly, carrying the baskets, enter from L. *Dandy follows. All
three are weary and downcast*

Polly (*calling wearily*) Firewood for sale! Only a shilling a bundle!
Firewood for sale!
Hughie Oh, save your breath Polly! No-one's goin' to buy any! (*He takes
her basket and drops it, with his own, upstage*)
Dandy (*to Polly, shaking his head and giving her the "thumbs down" sign*)

Woof!

Polly (*sighing*) I'm afraid you're right, Dandy. I can't understand it. We've never done anyone any harm. Why are they being so mean to us?

Hughie I dunno! They call me a lazy good-for-nothing. Well, the polite ones do! But I've had loads of jobs, haven't I?

Polly Hundreds!

Hughie Of course, what I really want to be is a singer! My voice is just as good as Michael Jackson's!!

Polly (*aside to the audience*) It's more like "Bubbles" really!

Hughie sings a few comic scales. Dandy covers his ears and howls

Hughie Cor! That's titivated me tonsils! I feel a song comin' on! Let's have another go at the old buskin'! We've got to raise some money somehow!

Polly I've just had an idea! Why don't we ask some of the boys and girls to help us.

Hughie Hey! What a brilliant idea!

Dandy barks in agreement

(*To the audience*) You'll help us, won't you kids? You'll come up and sing with us, won't you? Come on, don't be shy! Dandy won't bite you, unless you get near his teeth! No he's quite tame! Come on!

The House Lights go up. Polly and Dandy fetch children from the audience and take them on stage. They ask their names etc. Comic business with Dandy

(*To children*) Now, my little Pavagrotties, we want you to sing with us and earn some money to pay our rent. If anyone comes along you hold your hand out, like this! (*He demonstrates*) Just like Mum does to Dad on pay day! Now, what song would you like to sing? (*By-play with children. To pianist or conductor*) I don't think we've got that, have we, Mr/Mrs Lloyd Webber? No. We'll do this one. We all know that! Let's have a practice.

Song 4

Hughie and Polly encourage the children to sing. Comic business with Dandy listening to each one. They start the song again.

Several snooty villagers enter and cross the stage from R *to* L. *Hughie and Polly get the children to hold out their hands to them as they pass*

Hughie (*after song*) Thanks, kids! You didn't earn us any money but (*to the audience*) didn't they do well! (*He starts applause*)
Polly (*to the children; sadly*) We'd love to give you something for helping us, but we're so poor we haven't got a thing to give.

Dandy shakes his head sadly

The First Woman Villager enters L *carrying a bulging shopping bag*

First Woman (*to the audience, with disgust*) It's those horrible Hubbards! I shall ignore them! (*She sticks her nose in the air and starts to cross*)

Hughie intercepts her and raises his hat

Hughie Watch'er, gorgeous!
First Woman Let me pass!
Hughie What do you think of our little friends?
First Woman (*barely glancing at the children*) A horrid hoard of little hooligans!
Polly (*to her*) Would you like to hear them sing? They're very good.
First Woman Certainly not!

Dandy has crept up behind her and barks loudly

The woman screams, drops her bag, and runs out L

Hughie (*picking up the bag*) Oh, look what she's thrown away! (*To the children*) Now perhaps we can give you a prezzy! Let's 'ave a look!

He takes a pound of sausages from the bag and offers them to the children. He puts them back, takes out a toilet roll and offers that. He digs deeper and produces some packets of sweets. He hands them out. The children return to their seats. The House Lights go down

I wonder what's left?

They look in the bag

   Bread! Eggs!
Polly Baked beans!
Hughie Bacon!
Polly Air freshener?
Hughie That goes with the baked beans and sausages!
Dandy (*a delighted growl*)Sausages!
Hughie Coo! With this lot we can get Mum to do a smashin' fry-up!
Polly (*sadly*) I expect it'll be our last meal in the dear old cottage.

Magical music and the lighting changes slightly

   The Good Fairy, disguised in a long, tattered cloak with hood, hobbles
   on from R. *Fade magical music*

Hughie Hey! Look! It's (*topical gag*)!
Polly (*going to Fairy*) Hallo...

The Fairy backs off rather timidly

   Please don't be afraid. (*She helps the Fairy to* c) I'm Polly Hubbard.
   This is my brother, Hughie and that's our dog, Dandy.
Fairy (*in a frail, old voice*)
                              Oh, I've travelled a very long way,
                              And I haven't eaten for many a day!
                              The people I've met along the road,
                              Treat me like some repulsive toad!
                              I merely ask them for a little bread,
                              And they tell me to go and boil my head!
                              Oh, what a misery it is to be poor,
                              I'm sorry if I'm being a frightful bore.
Polly Not at all. We know all about poverty. We're being thrown out of
   our cottage because we can't pay the rent.
Hughie We've just had a bit of luck! We've got this bag full of goodies!
   Why don't you come home with us and share it?

Polly Yes, you're more than welcome to share what little we have.
Dandy (*nodding in agreement*) Woof!
Fairy How very kind— but are you sure? We've never even met before.
Polly You're poor, tired and hungry. That's all we need to know.

Fairy	Thank you for this act of charity,
	And I accept your kind hospitality.
Hughie	Our cottage is just along this street.
	And Mum'll give you something to soak your feet!

To suitable music, Polly, carrying the bag, helps the Fairy out L. Hughie follows with the baskets

Dandy (*to the audience, with a delighted growl*) Sausages!!

He scampers out after the others, as the Lights fade to Black-out

SCENE 3

Old Mother Hubbard's Cottage. Half set. Poverty in the best pantomime tradition! Crumbling plaster, sagging ceiling, broken windows with patched curtains etc. Back centre is a practical walk-in cupboard. The front door is R. Another entrance L

Mother Hubbard is discovered, pacing up and down in a very agitated state. She spots the audience and stops

Mother Oh, where's that Polly and Hughie? Fancy leaving their poor old Mother alone at a time like this! Alone, with me family seat all exposed and unprotected! Alone, and at the mercy of them blinkin' bailiffs! And they'll be back! Oh, you mark my words! I can feel it in me various veins!

A loud knock is heard at the front door. She jumps with fright

(*gulping*) I... I didn't 'ear that!

The knock is repeated

I didn't 'ear that, either!

The knock is repeated

It's them! It's them bailiffs! (*She creeps to the door and calls nervously*) Go away! I'm not in! I've emigrated to (*local place*)!
First Boy (*off* R) It's only us, Mother Hubbard!
Mother (*relieved*) Oh, it's just the kiddiwinks! (*She is about to unlock the door, then stops*) Suppose it's a trick! (*To the audience*) Shall I open the door?
Audience Yes!
Mother Shall I?
Audience Yes!
Mother Are you sure?
Audience Yes!
Mother (*bracing herself*) Right! 'ere goes! (*She unlocks the door*)

The children enter

Mother shuts the door after them, but forgets to lock it

Children Hallo, Mother Hubbard!
Mother Hallo, kids! Oh, you can't imagine what it's like bein' captive in yer own 'ome! I feel like something out of "Prisoner Cell Block H"! Have you seen Polly or Hughie anywhere?
First Girl No, and we haven't seen those bailiffs either!
First Boy We certainly scared them off!
Mother Don't be too sure! Oh, kids! If my 'usband were alive today, he'd be turnin' in 'is grave! (*Near to tears*) Oh, what a state of things! (*The children gather round to comfort her*)

Little Girl Cheer up! Remember, every silver lining has a cloud!

Mother gives her a double-take. The children burst into song

Song 5

First Boy (*after the song*) Can we go and play in your back garden, please?
Mother Of course you can, me dears! Make the most of the old place

while it's still mine. Go and 'ave a nice play! Come on, I'll unlock the back door for you.

She and the children exit L

A slight pause. The front door is slowly pushed open, and the First Bailiff sticks his head in. He peers about then tiptoes into the room

First Bailiff (*calling off* R) It's empty! Come on!
Second Bailiff (*off*) No fear!!

First Bailiff reaches outside and drags the Second Bailiff in. He shivers with fear and repulsion. First Bailiff shuts the door making the other jump

Second Bailiff Ahh... Ugh. Don't let anything touch me! I don't want to catch the dreaded lurgi!
First Bailiff I keep telling you, there isn't any lurgi! They made the whole thing up to scare us off. It was a trick!
Mother (*off* L) Enjoy yerselves, kids!
First Bailiff That's her! (*He takes out the order*) Ha! Ha! We'll get her this time! Let's hide! (*He looks around, sees the cupboard, and drags Second Bailiff into it with him*)

Mother enters L *and looks towards the front door*

Mother Oh, look! I never locked the front door! I am a silly old person, aren't I! Those bailiffs could get in. I'd better... (*She crosses to the door, then stops*) 'Ere! Did someone get in?
Audience Yes!
Mother Was it the bailiffs?
Audience Yes!
Mother (*thinking they're having fun with her*) Oh no it wasn't. You're just tryin' to give me the willies, you naughty lot! Oh yes, you are! *Etc., etc.*

During this exchange, the bailiffs emerge from the cupboard and creep up behind her. "Behind You" routine with audience. Mother turns to look and the Bailiffs keep behind her. Eventually, they come face to face. Mother yells and tries to make a get-away. Comic chase around the room, accompanied by "hurry" music. Finally they overpower her, force her to the floor and hold her down. Second Bailiff has his bottom sticking up, facing the front door

First Bailiff We win! Ha! Ha! (*He pushes the order under Mother's nose*) Mother Hubbard, it gives me great pleasure to present you with this eviction order!

Suddenly the front door bursts open and Dandy bounds in, followed by Hughie and Polly

Growling, Dandy makes straight for the Second Bailiff's bottom and rips the seat of his trousers out (a large Velcro-attached patch)

Screaming with fright, the Bailiffs run out through the open doorway

Hughie shuts the door and locks it. Dandy licks Mother's face as she lies on the floor

Mother Oy! Stop that! I've had one bath this week already!

Polly (*helping her up*) Are you all right, Mum? What were you doing on the floor with those two men?

Mother (*adjusting her dress*) Not what you're thinking! (*Aside to the audience*) Chance would be a fine thing! (*To Hughie*) Did you sell any firewood?

Hughie No. (*Brightly*) But we did get a bag full of groceries!

Mother (*excitedly*) A bag full of groceries! (*She rubs her hands*) Where is it?! Where is it?!

Hughie (*glumly*) We haven't got it anymore!

Dandy gives a dismal howl and shakes his head sadly

Mother You haven't ... What 'appened to it?

Polly We were bringin' it back home when this old beggar woman came along. She told us she hadn't eaten for days. Well, we took pity on her and invited her home to share the groceries. She said she was very tired, so we sat down under a tree to rest and...

Mother And?!

Polly Well... er... we all fell asleep...

Mother And?!

Polly When we woke up... the old woman had gone!

Hughie So had the bag of groceries! Sorry, Mum. Coo! I was really lookin' forward to a good old fry-up too! I'm so hungry I could eat a school dinner at (*local school*)!

Mother Well, you'll 'ave to stay 'ungry! There's not a scrap of food left in the 'ouse!

Dandy rubs his belly and whines

No, not even for you, my little dogsbody!

Dandy (*going to the cupboard and pointing to it*) Woof! Woof!

Hughie He thinks you've got a bone hidden in there!

Dandy nods and wags his tail. The others join Dandy at the cupboard. Mother on R, Hughie, Polly and Dandy on L

Mother Well, I'm sorry to disappoint you, my furry friend. There's nothing in there! It's empty! It's as bare as (*well-known bald person's*) head.

Dandy gives a growl

Oh, you don't believe Mummy?

Dandy shakes his head

Ooh! You cantankerous canine, you! Right! I'll prove it! I'll open the door and you can see for yourself!

She opens the cupboard door wide and faces front. In an eerie light, stands the motionless figure of the Good Fairy, still wearing the cloak. All see her, except Mother

There! I told you so! It's empty!

The others try to attract her attention, but she just babbles on to the audience

I don't know why I waste my breath! I told him it was empty and it is!
(*She looks in the cupboard, then back to the audience*) I've just about
had enough of...(*She stops, reacts, looks in the cupboard and does a
huge double take, then screams*) Ahhh!!!

Polly It's her! It's the old woman we told you about!

Mother The one who nicked the groceries?

Hughie ⎫
Polly ⎬ (*together*) ⎰ Yes.
Dandy ⎭   ⎱ Woof!

Mother (*getting her dander up*) Right! I'll soon sort 'er out! (*To Fairy*)
'Ere, you, missus! How dare you pinch my perishables! And ... and what
are you doin' in my cupboard?! What have you got to say for yerself?

The Good Fairy doesn't answer

Oh, I see! Dumb insolation, is it?! (*She rolls up her sleeves*) Well, I'm
goin' to make a citizen's arrest! Missus, you're nicked! (*She advances
on the Fairy*)

*There is a blinding flash, followed by a complete Black-out. The Fairy
drops her cloak and moves to* c. *Mother joins the others on* L

(*During Black-out*) Oh no. They've cut off me juice!!

*The Lights return to reveal the Good Fairy in all her shining magnifi-
cence. The others gape in awe*

Hughie Hey! How did Madonna get in 'ere?!

Fairy   I pray you do not be alarmed,
                   I am a being good and charmed,
                   You have no cause to be so wary,
                   I am here as your Good Fairy!

Mother   A Good Fairy! I must be dreamin'!!
                   I'll wake up soon all hot and steaming!

Polly   Mother, please don't interfere,
                   Just let her tell us why she's here.

Mother (*in a huff*) Oh, forgive me for breathin, I'm sure! (*To Fairy*)
                   Go then, Tinkerbell! You've got the floor!

Fairy   In the guise of a beggar I wandered this shire,
                   Dressed all in rags and looking most dire.
                   My aim was to find, in this secret fashion,
                   All those who would show just a little compassion.
                   My hopes of finding a good soul seemed blighted,
                   Until my eyes on these Hubbard children alighted!
                   Although poor themselves, with little to give,
                   They offered me food and somewhere to live.

She raises her arms and becomes really magical

                   So! By the powers of magic invested in me,
                   I grant you — one wish — for your kind charity!

Hughie (*thrilled*) A magic wish!! (*He whirls Polly around*) We've got
a magic wish! (*He whirls Mother around*) We've got a magic wish!

Mother Steady! Calm down! You know what 'appens when you get over-
excited!

Hughie Well, aren't you excited, Mum? Just think! We've got a magic
wish! We can have anything we ask for! Anything!

Mother (*petulantly*) It's got nothing to do with me! Fairy Liquid, over
there, gave you and Polly the wish. (*She starts to become weepy*) It
didn't include me! Not yer poor old 'ard-workin', down-on-her-luck
Mummy!

Polly Oh, Mum! We want you to have the wish! Don't we, Hughie!

Hughie Do we? ... Yes, of course, we do, Mum!

Polly You're the head of the family. You always make the decisions.

Hughie Yeah, you're the one who wears the trousers!

Mother (*aside to him*) Shut up, you twit! (*She indicates the audience*)
I've got 'em completely fooled! (*Aloud*) All right! You've twisted me
arm! I'll make the magic wish!

Polly What are you going to wish for?

Mother Oh, I dunno! One of them big, beefy "Chippendales" might be
nice!

Dandy Woof!!

Mother bends down and Dandy whispers in her ear

Mother (*shocked*) Certainly not! Bad doggie! (*To the audience*) 'E only
wants me to buy him shares in a poodle parlour! (*To Dandy*) You mucky

pup! (*She goes back to thinking*) Now, what shall I... Oh, dear! This is
very difficult...

Polly Just wish for something that will make you truly happy.

Mother (*thoughtfully; repeating Polly's words*) Something that will
make me truly happy... yes...yes! I know the very thing! My brother
Ossie! I'd love to see him again after all these years! That would make
me truly happy! Yes, that's it! (*To Fairy*) Right, your fairycake! 'Ere
goes! (*She clears her throat*) I wish that you take all four of us to my
brother Oswald — wherever he is!

Fairy   Your unselfish wish shall be a pleasure to grant,
                           All stand together, while I speak the magic chant!

They form a tight group down C. *The Fairy moves down* R

Mother (*to the audience*) Oh, this is just like bein' on "Surprise,
Surprise". (*To Fairy*) Go on, Cilla!

Fairy   To all powers of magic I now lay claim,
                           And will grant the wish of this goodly Dame!

She waves her wand. Magical music plays under. The stage grows dark.
Spotlights come up on the group and the Fairy

                           On Old Mother Hubbard I now cast my spell,
                           On Polly and Hughie and Dandy as well.
                           Transport them all safely to their destination,
                           And find brother Oswald's unknown location!

She points her wand at the group. There is a blinding flash, followed by
a complete Black-out

  The Fairy and Dandy exit under cover of darkness

The magical music becomes louder and more dramatic. Strange, weird
noises are heard. Mother and the others wail and call out as if they are
being transported through the air. The music and sounds continue into the
next scene

Scene 4

A prairie in the Wild, Wild West

Tabs or a frontcloth shows the dusty, sun-baked prairie with mountains in the distance. In the foreground are a few cacti and the sun-bleached bones of a cow

There is a flash and the scene is revealed. The music and sounds fade out. Mother, Polly and Hughie are discovered in a tangled heap on the ground. They have evidently just landed!

Mother (*groaning at the bottom of the heap*) Mmm!...Ooo! .... Ger off! ... Ah! You've got yer dirty great foot in me ear 'ole... Ger off !!

Polly and Hughie disentangle themselves and stagger to their feet

(*Sitting up; very dishevelled and dazed*) Well, don't just stand there! 'Elp me up!

They do so

'Ere! Where's me parlour?! Where's me cottage?! Where's the village?!!
Polly We're here, Mum! The Fairy granted your wish. This must be where Uncle Ossie lives!
Mother (*looking about her*) What 'ere?! But it's ... it's just a dried up *dessert*! Just look at it!

They come forward and peer out at the audience

There's nothing as far as the eye can see! Nothing, but them funny little cactus things and a few old lumps of rock! Not a house! Not a "Happy Eater"! And not a single human being in sight!
Hughie (*peering*) She's right there!
Mother Oh, whatever can Ossie be doin' in a place like this? Where do you think we are?
Polly I have a feeling it's ... it's America!
Mother What?!! With all them cowboys an' Indians?!

Hughie (*pointing to the cow's skull*) Look at that!

Mother (*looking and yelling*) Ahh! It's Norman Tebbit!

Hughie It's just a pile of old bones. Dandy'll be happy! He can have his own private take-away! (*Suddenly concerned*) Hey! Where is Dandy?!!

Mother ⎞
Polly ⎬   (*together*) Dandy! Here, boy!*Etc, etc!*
Hughie ⎠

Mother (*to the audience*) Come on, you can help call him!

They get the audience to call for Dandy a couple of times

Hughie Shh!!

They listen. Silence

Polly I can't hear him barking. (*To the audience*) Can you?

Audience No!

Hughie Let's look over there!

They exit R calling "Dandy! Here boy, etc."

A slight pause. Tex Laramie is heard singing off L

He enters, followed by several cowboys and cowgirls. If possible, one could be playing a guitar and another a mouth organ

Song 6

After the song, the cowboys and cowgirls bid farewell to Tex and exit L

Barking is heard, and Dandy bounds on from R. He stops dead in his tracks at the sight of Tex and exits L

Mother (*off R*) I heard his bark!... Over this way!

Mother, Polly and Hughie run on from R. They too stop dead in their tracks at the sight of Tex. Dandy joins them

Tex (*with an affable wave*) Howdy, strangers!

Polly (*moving to greet him*) Hallo...

Mother (*pulling her back*) Polly! I told you never to talk to strange men! (*To the audience*) And they don't come much stranger! (*To Hughie*) You're the nearest thing we've got to a man — you talk to him! Ask him to give you his particulars!

Hughie His what?

Mother (*pushing him over to Tex*) Go on!!

Hughie (*to Tex ; nervously*) Er... Nice year we're havin' for the time of the weather!

Tex roars with laughter

Mother (*pushing Hughie aside*) Oh, you useless great article! Get out of the way! I'll do the talkin'!!

Hughie That'll make a nice change!

Mother (*to Tex*) Now, then, young man! Who are you and what do you want?

Tex roars with laughter again

Mother (*to the audience*) Easy to please, isn't he?! I wish he was out there with you lot! (*To Tex*) What's the joke?

Tex Fergive me fer laughin', ma'am! But you folks sure do talk mighty funny!

Mother (*to the audience; dismayed*) We do? (*To Tex*) Listen, never mind our electrocution — who are you?

Tex The name's Tex Laramie, ma'am! I'm plumb delighted to make yer acquaintance. (*He removes his hat and gives her a sweeping bow*)

Mother (*flattered and overcome*) Oo! (*To the audience*) Oh, I think I'm in with a chance, girls! (*To Tex*) I'm Mother Hubbard — a widow! (*She flutters her eyelashes at him*) Some call me Old Mother Hubbard — I can't think why, can you? (*She preens herself*)

Polly (*pushing in, eager to be introduced*) Er...

Mother (*annoyed at the intrusion*) This is my daughter — with no manners! Polly.

Tex (*offering his hand*) Howdy, Miss Polly.

Polly (*taking it*) How do you do.

Tex (*really carried away at the sight of her*) Shucks! If you ain't the purtiest gal I ever did see!

Mother (*to the audience*) Bang goes my chances!
Polly Thank you, Mr Laramie.
Tex Say! Call me Tex!
Polly Thank you — Tex.

*They gaze adoringly into each other's eyes for some time. Comic reactions
from Mother, Hughie and Dandy*

Hughie (*aside to Mother*) Shall we have the interval now?
Mother (*pulling Hughie between Tex and Polly*) This is my son, Hughie!
Tex Howdy, Hughie!

He gives Hughie a very firm handshake. Dandy makes himself known

Mother And this is Dandy.

Dandy sits up and holds out his paw to Tex

Tex (*shaking his paw*) Howdy, feller!
Polly (*to Tex*) Can you tell us exactly where we are?
Tex I sure can. You're two miles from Deadman's Gulch!
Polly (*to Tex*) Is it a town?
Tex Sure it's a town! Only town in these here parts! (*Puzzled*) Say! Where
    do you folks hail from? What yuh doin' way out here in the middle of
    the prairie anyhow? Did yuh git thrown off the stage?
Mother No, but it could 'appen at any moment!
Polly I think he means a stage coach, Mum.
Mother Oh! (*To Tex*) We came 'ere to find someone.
Tex An' who might that be?
Hughie Our Uncle Ossie!
Mother My dear brother. Mr Oswald Hubbard. Do you know him?
Tex Nope! I don't reckon I do, ma'am.
Mother He looks a lot like me! Only not so young and with it. Are you
    sure?
Tex I guess I'd remember him if he looked anythin' like you, ma'am.
    (*Aside, he makes a wry face at the audience*)
Polly We have it on good authority that he's here somewhere.
Tex Wull, I only bin in these parts a short while. But I reckon my sidekick
    might know yer uncle. Yep! Old Tumbleweed knows just about every

critter in this here territory!
Tumbleweed (*off* L) Yee-hah!
Tex Here he comes now!

Tumbleweed enters from L. He is a bewhiskered, dust-covered, disreputable old son-of-a-gun

Hughie You can't fool us! It's Jeremy Beadle!
Tex (*to the others*) Folks! I want y'all to meet old Tumbleweed!
Tumbleweed (*waving to them*) Howdy, folks! (*He waves to the audience*) Howdy, pardn'rs! I'm as sure as shootin' pleased to meet y'all! Yes, siree!! (*He spits off stage* L)

A bell rings off stage L

Tex Old timer, this is the Hubbard family.

Tumbleweed peers across at them. He sees Mother and obviously likes what he sees

Tumbleweed (*aside to Tex*) Say, Tex! Be hintroducin' me to that purty little filly over thar!
Tex (*introducing Polly*) This is Miss Polly...
Tumbleweed Not her! T'other one! (*He leers*) The bigger one!
Tex That's Mother Hubbard.

Tumbleweed ambles across to Mother. He hitches up his belt, and gives her an enormous wink. Mother reacts

Tumbleweed Howdy, ma'am! (*He whips off his filthy hat and showers her with dust*)

She coughs and splutters. He slaps her on the back, almost knocking her over

Dad-burn it! If you ain't a sight fer these sore ole eyes o' mine!
Mother Eyes?! (*To the audience*) First time I saw an overgrown hedge with eyes!
Tumbleweed (*looking her up and down*) You sure do put me in mind of

a gal I once nuw! Same cute little nose! Same pearly white teeth! Same
slender little neck! Same ....

Mother We'll stop at the neck, if you don't mind!

Tumbleweed She sure was mighty purty! Clementina, that was her name!

Mother A ladyfriend?

Tumbleweed Nope! A mule I once had!

*Mother reacts. He bursts out laughing and slaps his thigh making the dust
rise*

Mother (*to the audience; coughing*) Oh! Where's the "Shake 'n' Vac"?

Tumbleweed (*producing a pouch and offering it to her*) Chaw o'baccy?

Mother (*revolted*) No, ta! I prefer "Tic-Tacs" !!

Tumbleweed (*producing a bottle and offering that*) Slug o' red eye?

Mother Not between meals! (*Eager be rid of him*) Why don't you go and
talk to Dandy. You can swap shaggy dog stories!

Tex Tumbleweed, these folk need yer help. They're lookin' fer one o'
their kinfolk. Feller by the name of Oswald Hubbard. You ever hear of
him?

Tumbleweed Oswald Hubbard? Why, sure I heered of him!

Delighted, the others gather round him with mounting enthusiasm

He come out frum old England years ago!

Others Yes?!!

Tumbleweed Struck a rich vein too!

Others Yes?!!

Tumbleweed Made a packet!

Others Yes?!!

Tumbleweed Lost it gamblin' !!

Others (*deflated*) No?!!

Tumbleweed But he kept enough to buy the "Lazy B" ranch!

Others Oooo!!

Tumbleweed An' it's the biggest spread hereabouts!

The Hubbards and Dandy dance for joy

Mother Hurray!! (*She bends over to speak to the pianist/ conductor*) Did
you 'ear that?! My brother's got the biggest spread hereabouts!

Tumbleweed (*eyeing her posterior*) An' you ain't doin' so bad yerself —
tharabouts! (*He gives her a playful slap on the rear*)

She reacts and he hoots with laughter

Polly (*to Tumbleweed*) Will you take us to Uncle Ossie's ranch?
Tumbleweed Yep!
Others Great!
Tumbleweed Won't do yuh no good though!
Others Why not?
Tumbleweed 'Cos he ain't there no more! 'Bout a year ago he ups an'
disappears! Reeel mysterious like! He ain't bin seen since!
Mother But ... but what about 'is ranch? The "Lazy Layabout" ...or
whatever it's called?
Tumbleweed The day after yer brother disappears, Matt Vinyl an' his
boys took over the place!
Hughie Matt who?
Tumbleweed Matt Vinyl!! (*Getting worked up*) He's the meanest,
mangiest, peskiest sidewinder in the territory!
Mother You don't like him then?
Tumbleweed Like him?!! Dad-burn it! I hate the lowdown, yeller bellied,
son of a ...
Mother Yes! We get the picture!
Polly Tex, do you think this Matt Vinyl had something to do with our
uncle's disappearance?
Tex I reckon so. He runs Deadman's Gulch now! If there's any dirty work
goin' on, you kin bet yer bottom dollar Matt Vinyl's at the back of it!
Tumbleweed You sure can! (*He spits*)

A bell rings off stage R

Mother (*to the audience*) I hope you've brought umbrellas! (*To others*)
Right! Come on, we're going to Deadman's Gulch!
Tex What you plannin' to do thar, ma'am?
Mother I'm goin' to find out what this Matt Emulsion's done with my
brother Ossie! I'll soon sort 'im out!
Tex I wouldn't advise that, ma'am. Vinyl is a mighty dangerous
customer!
Mother I'll get the law on 'im!

Tumbleweed (*hooting with laughter*) Hee! Hee! Hee!

Mother (*to the audience*) Look out! He's goin' to lay an egg!

Tumbleweed Thar ain't no law in Deadman's Gulch! Vinyl shot 'em all! (*He jabs a finger at Mother*) Bang!! Bang!! He'll do the same to you if yuh cross him. You'll end up with more holes than a dawg's got fleas!

Dandy reacts

Mother But we've got to find out what's 'appened to Ossie!

Polly Can't you help us, Tex?

Tex Wull, there might be a way. If you're willin' to put yerselves in my hands.

Polly (*eagerly*) Oh, yes!

Mother Steady, girl, steady!

Tex I'll take y'all into town. Let on you're jist visitin' kinfolk o' mine. That way we kin find out things without raisin' Vinyl's suspicions. What you say? Are yuh game?

The Hubbards look at each other and come to a unanimous decision

Hughie ⎫
Mother ⎬ (*together; to Tex*) ⎰ Yep!
Polly ⎪
Dandy ⎭   ⎱ Woof!

Tex OK! First thing we gotta do is git you outta them clothes.

Tumbleweed (*nudging Mother and winking*) Yep!

Tex Dressed in them duds you'll stick out like a one-legged man at a butt kickin' party! Tumbleweed, we'll stop off at our cabin an' git 'em fitted out. Western style!

He offers Polly his arm and leads her out L. *Dandy offers Hughie his arm and they follow*

Tumbleweed leers at Mother and offers his arm

Tumbleweed You jist mosey right along with me, ma'am! (*He winks*)

Mother (*to the audience, grimacing*) Just my flippin' luck to be fancied by a moth-eaten old mountain goat!

Tumbleweed Gol-darn it! I luvs it when you talks purty! Yes, sireee! (*He spits*)

The sound of shattering glass is heard and all the Lights go out. Black-out

Scene 5

The Town of Deadman's Gulch

Full set. A typical street in a typical rough, tough Wild West town. Livery stable, feed store, "Wells Fargo" depot, etc. Prominent on L is the " Silver Dollar Saloon". It is brightly painted and has practical swing doors. On R is the Sheriff's Office. This is boarded up and has a notice on the door that reads " Closed ownin' to lead poisonin'"

Cowboys, cowgirls and the townsfolk are discovered, going straight into a rip-roaring Wild West song and dance

Song 7

After the song, harsh laughter is heard coming from the saloon. A man crashes backwards through the swing doors and rolls over in the street. Hank and Jake, the cause of his propulsion, follow him out, roaring with laughter. Matt Vinyl enters from the saloon, carrying a collecting tin. He strides over to the man, who cowers on the ground

Vinyl That'll teach you to come collectin' fer charity in my saloon! (*He reads the label on the tin*) "Give generously to the poor widders an' orphans"! Ha listen, Mister! I made most of 'em widders an' orphans! An' I ain't payin' fer no privilege!

Hank and Jake hoot with laugher

(*To them*) Boys! Here's yer pocket money fer the week!

He throws them the tin and they eagerly try to prise it open. The man staggers to his feet

Man Hey ! Stop! You can't do that! That money's fer the deservin'!
Vinyl Well, they look mighty deservin' to me! (*He gives a sneering laugh*)

Laughing, Hank and Jake succeed in opening the tin and share out the money. The man rushes across but Vinyl grabs him by the lapels

    Say! How old are you, Mister?
Man Forty! (*or whatever*)
Vinyl D'you wanta live to be forty-one?

He whips out his gun and thrusts it under the man's nose. Hank and Jake hoot with laughter. Vinyl pushes the man to the ground again

Hank (*throwing the empty tin to the man*) Here! Try yer luck some place!
Vinyl Yeah! Why don't yuh try (*local place*)! (*To the audience, sneering*)
    Thar's a lotta pesky do-gooders thar! I hear they're a bunch of low-
    down, mangy little creeps! Is that right?!
Audience No!!
Vinyl Oh, yes, yuh are!

"Oh, no, we're not!" routine with audience

Threateningly, Vinyl pulls out his gun and points it around the audience. Before returning it to its holster, he flamboyantly attempts to twirl the gun around his finger. He makes a complete mess of it! Hank, Jake and the crowd roar with laughter

    (*Bellowing at the crowd*) Git outta here! (*He fires the gun into the air*)

The crowd scatter and run out in all directions

Hank and Jake cling to each other, helpless with laughter. Vinyl reacts and pushes them apart. He knocks their hats off. As they bend to pick them up, he kicks them in the seat of their pants

    No-one laughs at Black Matt Vinyl! The Most Feared Man in The West!
    No-one! (*To the audience*) An' that goes fer you as well! If I catch any
    of you pesky little varmints laughin' at me. I'll fill yuh full o' lead! Oh,
    yes I will! (*By-play with audience; to Hank and Jake*) Now I gotta do
    somethin' to git back my respect in this town! Somethin' that'll make
    'em all hate an' loathe me again!
Hank I got it! Cancel the flower show!

Vinyl We ain't got no flower show!

Hank Wull, organize one, an' then cancel it!

Vinyl (*hand on gun*) I'll cancel you in a minute, knucklehead!

Jake Hey, boss! Why don't yuh stop sellin' crisps in the saloon!

Vinyl Are you crazy! What am I gonna do with them fifty boxes of "Barbecued Buffalo" flavour I got in just las' week?! No, it's gotta be sonethin' reel mean! I'm the baddie around here, an' I gotta keep up appearances!

Song 8

An "evil" comedy song and dance for Vinyl and two sidekicks. They dance into the saloon, jeering at the audience as they go

A commotion is heard and the crowd enter excitedly from both sides. Tex and Polly enter at the back. Polly now wears a very becoming cowgirl costume

Tex (*to crowd; leading Polly down* c) Howdy, folks!

Crowd Howdy, Tex!

Tex I'd like y'all to meet my visitin' kinfolk. This is Miss Polly.

Crowd Howdy, Miss Polly!

Polly (*slightly embarrassed*) How do you...er... Howdy!

Tex (*clearing to* L *with Polly*) An' here comes the rest!

Hughie and Dandy enter at the back. Hughie wears a comic cowboy outfit with a huge stetson and enormous fur chaps. He carries a lasso. He is trying to be the macho cowboy and walking à la John Wayne, with disastrous results

Tex This is Dandy and Hughie!

Crowd Howdy, Dandy!

Dandy Woof!!

Crowd Howdy, Hughie!

Hughie (*with an appalling accent*) How-de-do-dee, partn'rs! Yipee! Git off yer horse an' drink yer milk! Let's git them wagons in a circle an' rope them thar steers! Yipee! (*He tries to twirl the lasso and gets in a hopeless tangle*)

Dandy struts off L *and returns immediately, expertly twirling a trick lasso above his head*

The crowd cheer and clap. Dandy bows to them letting the lasso drop and revealing the trick. All laugh. He and Hughie join the others on L

Mother (*off; yelling*) Ger off! Don't touch what you can't afford. Oh!!

She runs on at the back, hotly pursued by Tumbleweed. She now wears an outrageous cowgirl costume with masses of fringing and rhinestones. Tumbleweed is trying to adjust the fringing on her short skirt

(*Pushing him away*) Will you stop doin' that you infuriatin' fur ball, you! If I want my dangly bits rearranged I'll do it meself! Go away and leave me alone!

Tumbleweed (*chuckling*) Hee! Hee! You can't put me off, honey lamb! I bin a prospector all my life! I'm used to diggin' and scrapin' an' scratchin' till I hit pay dirt!

Mother I've got news for you! You hit dirt a long time ago!

Tumbleweed I kin be as stubborn as a mule and I got the skin of a rhinoceros!

Mother Keep your family out of this!

Tumbleweed (*sidling up and leering at her*) When I gits a hankerin' fer somethin' — I sure gits it!

Mother (*showing her fist*) You'll get this in yer cake 'ole in a minute! Oh, go away and play with yer panhandle, if you want something to do!

Tumbleweed Dad-burn it! You sure likes playin' hard to git! Yes, siree!

He gives her a playful slap on the bottom. She wallops him and knocks him to the ground. The crowd roar with laughter

(*Sitting up, dazed but delighted*) Dang my breeches! How I luvs that little woman!

Mother (*to the audience*) I can understand his fascination though, can't you girls? (*She preens herself*) This new outfit is enough to turn any man's stomach... I mean head! Oh, yes! Do you like it? 'Ere, who said I look like a giant lampshade?! No, I think it really does something for me! I feel like a cross between Dolly Parton, the Lone Ranger an' last year's Christmas tree! Oh, yes I'm sure I could get used to this rough, tough Wild West! A place where men are men, and women are ... glad of it!!

Song 9

A lively foot tapping "Hoe-down" type song and dance, involving every-one

When it is in full swing, Matt Vinyl enters from the saloon, followed by Hank and Jake

He sees what is going on, pulls out his gun and fires it into the air. The music and merriment stop abruptly

The crowd scatter and run out in all directions

Vinyl What's all the commotion about?! Nobody asked my permission fer singin' an' dancin!! (*He looks Mother up and down*) Say! When did the circus hit town?

He and his sidekicks guffaw

Mother (*aside to Tex*) Who's the buffoon in the black bonnet?
Tex (*aside to her*) That's him! (*Aside to all*) That's Matt Vinyl!

They react

Jist leave the talkin' to me.(*He goes to Vinyl*) Howdy, Vinyl!
Vinyl (*sneering*) Howdy, yerself!
Tex (*indicating the others*) These here are visitin' kinfolk o' mine from out East.
Vinyl (*with suspicion*) Oh, yeah!

He circles around Mother. She reacts

From out East, huh? (*He snaps at Mother*) East o' where?!
Mother Er... (*local place*)!
Vinyl (*growling*) Never heard of it!
Mother (*growling back*) You're lucky!
Vinyl D'you know who I am?! (*He strikes the "gunfighter" pose with*

hands out at sides and his legs wide apart)
Mother A man who's had an accident?
Vinyl I'm Matt Vinyl! I've killed more men than you've had hot dinners!
Mother (*preening herself*) Oh! You an' me could form a club!
Vinyl I run this town!
Mother Oh, like (*local personality*), you mean?
Vinyl Around here I'm known as a big shot!
Mother A big what!
Vinyl Shot!
Mother Oh shot, I thought you said a big... er... so, you're the big cheese, are you?
Vinyl (*puffing himself up*) I sure am!
Mother Good, I wondered where that awful smell was comin' from! (*She sniffs him and grimaces*) Phew!

The others laugh including Hank and Jake. Enraged,Vinyl hits them both with his hat

Vinyl (*to Mother; threateningly*) Listen, you! Don't make fun of Matt Vinyl!
Mother Oh, I wouldn't dream of it! It looks lovely on my bathroom walls!
Vinyl If you've come here thinkin' you kin throw yer weight about — fergit it! This town ain't big enough fer the two of us!
Mother No, you could do with losin' a few pounds!
Vinyl Why, you old...

He raises his fist to her but Dandy growls at him and he backs off

Tex We ain't lookin' fer no trouble, Vinyl!
Vinyl Jist make sure you ain't!

He moves to.Hank and Jake DL. The others "freeze" and the stage grows dark. Green spotlight on Vinyl and his two cronies

Hank Hey, boss! I bin thinkin'!!
Vinyl What with?
Hank That ole woman — don't she remind you o' someone?
Vinyl Yeah, Freddy Krueger's (*or other TV/ film ugly*) granny!
Hank No, don't she remind you o' that English fella, that Oswald

Hubbard! The one who had the "Lazy B" ranch?

Jake Yuh mean, the one we... (*He mimes hitting someone several times*)

Hank Yeah!

Vinyl Mm... Yeah! I reckon you could be right, Hank! There is a certain likeness!

Jake You figger they've come alookin' fer him, boss?

Vinyl (*sneering*) Wull, they ain't gonna find him! The buzzards took care of that! (*Grisly laugh*) But they might be here to stir up trouble. We've gotta find out what their game is! If they're lookin' fer trouble I'll give 'em one-way tickets to Boot Hill! (*To the audience*) An' that goes fer any of their friends!

They sneer at the audience and slap their holsters. The lighting returns to normal. The others "unfreeze"

Vinyl and his boys look at them, roar with evil laughter and exit into the saloon

Tex Now yuh kin see what a lowdown sidewinder we're up against!

Mother I don't care how low his winders are, he'll not stop me findin' brother Ossie!

Dandy (*in agreement*) Woof! Woof!

Hughie We're right behind you, Mum!

Tumbleweed (*literally*) We sure are!

She jumps, reacts and pushes him away

Polly Having seen what sort of person he is, there's no doubt that Vinyl had something to do with Uncle Ossie's disappearance. But how are we going to prove it?

Tex Let me figger that out. Meantime, don't do anythin' to raise his suspicions—jist act dumb. (*To Hughie*) Can you do that?

Mother He's an expert!

Tex An' above all, don't tell anyone who yuh are, or why yur here! (*To Mother*) Now, ma'am, why don't we finish off that little ole song an' dance!

Mother Sure thin', partn'r! Head 'em up, an' move 'em out! Yippeee!!

Reprise of Song 9

The crowd enter and join the song and dance. Comic finish with Mother sitting on Tumbleweed's knee and both collapsing to the ground. On the last note of music——

— the CURTAIN *falls*

ACT II

Scene 1

The Silver Dollar Saloon. Full set. A gaudy fun palace as seen in a thousand Wild West films. Back LC are practical swing doors, with a view of the street beyond. L is the bar. Tables and chairs up RC. Entrances R and L. If possible, a honky-tonk piano DR, complete with bowler-hatted pianist

Old Tumbleweed, cowboys, male townsfolk and saloon "ladies" are discovered in raucous merriment. A bartender is busy behind the bar. As soon as the scene is set, everyone breaks into a rowdy song

Song 10

After the song, they all whoop and cheer. The bartender bangs the bar and yells for silence. The crowd sit at the tables and clear to the sides

Bartender (*announcing*) An' now — fer yur edification an' delight! — the Silver Dollar Saloon proudly presents — Miss Lulabelle an' her dancin' darlin's! (*To pianist on stage or in the pit*) Hit it, professor!

The music strikes up, and the male clientele clap, whoop and stamp their feet

    Miss Lulabelle, followed by a troupe of shapely dancers, parade on from R. They strike a pose, then go into their dance routine

Dance 10A

During the dance, Old Tumbleweed tries to join in and makes a comic nuisance of himself

He is roughly ejected through the swing doors by the bartender

The dance ends with a tableau and the crowd clap and cheer

The dancers parade off L

Miss Lulabelle remains by the bar

Two loud shots are heard off R. *The crowd fall silent, and look with dread towards the sound*

Matt Vinyl strides on from R, *blowing down the barrel of his gun*

Vinyl (*calling off* R) Take him to the undertakers, boys! (*To the audience*) Ha! That'll teach folks to ask fur soft paper in my gents room! (*He twirls his gun and puts it away; to the crowd*) What's got into you?! Ain't this a saloon?! Enjoy yerselves! (*To the pianist*) Play somethin'!!

The piano plays quietly under the following. The crowd talk together in hushed tones. Vinyl moves down RC, *nods to Lulabelle who slinks across to join him*

I want yuh to do somethin' fur me, Lulabelle. It's about them strangers in town.
Lulabelle Tex Laramie's kinfolk, yuh mean?
Vinyl Ha! If they're his kinfolk, you're Snow White! Listen, I figger they're up to no good. I want you to find out who they really are, an' what they're doin' here. There's a young fella called Hughie. He oughta be a pushover to someone with your ... er... persuasive little ways!

They chuckle. The piano music fades out

Lulabelle (*preening herself*) Just leave him to me!

Off stage Hughie is heard whistling the theme from " The Good, the Bad and the Ugly". A hush falls and everyone looks towards the swing doors

Hughie swaggers into view. He is still trying to portray the tough cowboy. He goes to push open the doors, but finds them stuck. He has to crawl underneath. He tries the doors again and they open. He gives them a hefty push outwards and turns to face the room. The doors swing inwards and knock him flat on his face. The crowd roar with laughter

Vinyl (*to Lulabelle*) That's him! He's all yours!

He exits R *laughing*

Hughie picks himself up and resumes his swagger

Hughie (*to the crowd, in deep macho tones*) Howdy!
Crowd Howdy!
Hughie (*to the audience, in same tones*) Howdy!

They answer

    (*Then as himself*) It's me, folks! (*He swaggers to the bar and goes to lean on it. He misses and falls over*)

The crowd roar with laughter

He hauls himself up so his chin is resting on the top bar

Bartender (*growling at him*) Howdy!!

Hughie jumps with fright and falls backwards. Roars of laughter. Getting up, he swaggers to the bar again

    What's yur poison, Mister?
Hughie (*in deep, mean tones*) Give me... Give me two fingers of...(*as himself*) low-alcohol rot gut, please.

The crowd laugh

    (*To them*) Well, I'm riding!

Lulabelle slinks across and moves in very close to Hughie at the bar

Lulabelle (*at her seductive best*) Howdy, Handsome!

Hughie (*gulping at the sight of her*) Er ...Hallo, Mrs Woman!

Lulabelle The name's Lulabelle.

Hughie Oh, that's got a nice ring to it!

Lulabelle (*to barman*) Give this gentleman a big drink. (*To Hughie*) Have it on me.

Hughie Don't be silly! You'll get all wet!

The bartender fills up a very large glass and presents it to Hughie. He reacts

(*To the barman*) Have you got a snorkle an' a pair of flippers to go with this?! (*He puts the glass on the bar*)

Lulabelle (*slipping her arm through his and leading him to* C) Say Handsome! Let's go some place private an' talk. I wanta git to know you better. You're new!

Hughie Yes, but I'm not fresh!

A commotion is heard from outside. Hank and Jake come through the swing doors. They are dragging the struggling figure of Little Deer, an attractive young Indian maiden. They pull her down LC

Little Deer (*fighting like a wild cat*) Let um go!... Me hate um you!... Let um go!

She bites Hank's hand. With a yell, he releases her and nurses his hand. She kicks Jake on the shin. With a yelp, he lets her go and hops about in agony

You no touch um me again (*Proudly*) Me, Little Deer! Daughter of Big Chief Thunder Cloud!

Jake and Hank advance on her

Hank Why, you pesky redskin, I'll ...

Lulabelle (*intervening*) Hold it, boys, hold it! (*To Little Deer*) Who'd you say you was?

Little Deer Me Little Deer! Father — Big Chief Thunder Cloud!

Hank We found her sneakin' around outside!

Lulabelle What are you doin' in Deadman's Gulch? You know Injuns ain't allowed in town.

Little Deer Me only come listen to music. Music from big box with many teeth!

Lulabelle (*puzzled*) Box with many teeth? (*She realizes and laughs*) Oh, she means the piano!

Little Deer nods enthusiastically and mimes playing a piano

Little Deer Heap good music! Plenty def beat.

Lulabelle (*to pianist*) Say, professor! You gotta fan at last!

The pianist plays a little. Little Deer is thrilled to bits

Hank Let's throw her out!

He and Jake advance on Little Deer but Hughie plants himself in their way

Hughie (*playing the heavy*) Say! You touch her an' I'll...

Jake (*growling at him*) You'll what?!!

Hughie (*gulping and losing his nerve*) I'll ... I'll scream the place down! Don't be such party poopers! She can stay and listen to the music if she wants to!

Hank Oh, no she can't!

Hughie Oh, yes she can! (*To the audience*) Can't she, kids?!

Audience Yes!

Hank ⎫ (*together; to the audience*)   Oh, no, she can't!
Jake ⎭

Routine with audience. Finally Hughie calls a halt to it

Hughie (*to Lulabelle*) If Miss Little Deer goes, so do I! I'll take my custom elsewhere! I've been thrown out of better places than this! The (*local pub or hotel*) to name but one!

Lulabelle pulls Hank and Jake aside and whispers quickly to them. Little Deer moves closer to Hughie and they exhange bashful glances

Lulabelle (*to Hughie*) OK, Handsome. Jist fer you she kin stay an' listen

to the music fur a short spell. But you stick around! I shall be comin'
back to see you sometime!

She winks at him and exits R pushing Hank and Jake out in front of her

Again Hughie and Little Deer exchange bashful glances

Hughie (*to Little Deer*) You... You like listening to music, then?
Little Deer (*nodding*) Me like um.
Hughie Me like um too! Don't they have any music where you come
from?
Little Deer (*glumly*) Only drum! (*She makes the sound of a solemn drum
beat*) Boom, boom, boom, boom! Boom, boom, boom, boom! All um
time! Heap big boring!
Hughie Do they have dancing?!
Little Deer (*glumly again*) Only war dance. (*She comically demonstrates
a solemn dance*) Heap big boring too!
Hughie Oh, where I come from there's all sorts of music an' dancing!
You'd love it! Look, I'll show you!

Song 11

*He starts the song, then encourages Little Deer to join in. The crowd take
up the song as Hughie teaches Little Deer the dance steps. It ends with
them in an embrace, gazing adoringly at each other*

The crowd tip-toe out, leaving them alone

Little Deer Me like um you.
Hughie Me like um you too!
Little Deer What um you called?
Hughie Me called um Hughie.
Little Deer (*having difficulty pronouncing it*) Huuu ... eee!

They both giggle

Me Little Deer.
Hughie You can say that again! (*He takes her hand and swings it
bashfully*) Little Deer, can I... can I walk you home?

Little Deer (*suddenly very serious*) Heap bad medicine! My father, he Big Chief! He much angry if um see me with Pale Face! He blow um top! (*Sadly*) Me go now! (*She moves up to swing doors*)

Hughie (*following her*) But can we see each other again?!

Little Deer Me not sure! Old Indian saying say "Buffalo may love porcupine, but in end one of them get um hurt"!

She quickly kisses him on the cheek and runs out through the swing doors

Hughie (*to the audience, over the moon*) She kissed me! She kissed me! Oh! I'm in love! (*He hugs himself and waltzes around*) Oh, Little Deer! Little Deer!

As he does this, Lulabelle enters from R and slinks over to him. He waltzes right into her and falls over

Lulabelle Hallo again, Big Boy!

Hughie (*to the audience, sitting up*) Oh, no! It's the Venus Fly Trap again! (*He scrambles to his feet and makes to leave*) I'm off!

Lulabelle (*grabbing him and pulling him close*) What's the rush, honey lamb! I told you I wanted to git better acquainted.

Hughie Must dash. I've got to mosey on down to the Ole Corral an' rope me a steer!

He manages to pull free and backs away from her as she stalks him. He backs into the bar

Lulabelle Say, you ain't touched yur drink! (*She leans right across him to pick up the glass*) Go on, drink it! It'll put hairs on yur chest! (*She takes the glass and has a tiny sip*) All of it!

Hughie (*to the audience*) A man's gotta do what a man's gotta do! (*He holds his nose and drains the glass. He nonchalantly throws it behind the bar. He smacks his lips, pleasantly surprised*) Mm! It's nice! A bit like...(*Suddenly the drink hits him. He pulls his hat down, goes cross-eyed and his legs turn to rubber. He chokes and looks as if he's going to explode*)

Lulabelle Now we can talk.

Hughie shakes his head, then fans his tongue with his hat. Lulabelle leads him to c. *He is very wobbly and has difficulty focussing*

Now, tell Lulabelle all about yurself. What are yo doin' in Deadman's Gulch?

Hughie (*blasé with drink*) Oooh! Thash eashy peashy! Hic! We're in Gedman's Dulch to find out... (*He suddenly remembers, sways away from her, and puts his fingers to his lips*) Shh! (*To the audience, giggling*) Whoops! I nearly let the bag out of the cat, didn't I! Mush'ent tell anyone! (*To Lulabelle*) Ish a shecret! My slips are lealed! Hic!

Lulabelle Oh, you're the strong, silent type, huh?

Hughie (*a loud whisper*) Thash me! (*A very loud belch*) Burp!

Lulabelle (*moving close and stroking his chin*) But you kin tell Lulabelle all yur secrets. They won't go no further. I'm like a sealed book.

Hughie. You look more like a shet of enshyclopediash to me!

Lulabelle Come on, Big Boy! Let's git active!!

Dance 12

Lulabelle grabs Hughie and draws him into a comic seductive dance. In his stupefied state, he is dragged along and thrown about like a rag doll. It ends with Lulabelle bending him over in a "Valentino" type embrace. She lets him go and he crashes to the floor. He crawls to the bar, climbs on to it and curls up, ready for sleep

(*Rushing over and prodding him*) Hey! Wake up, Sleepin' Beauty! You ain't told me what I wanta know yet! (*She shakes him roughly*)

Hughie (*half asleep*) Tell me a story, Mummy!

Lulabelle You tell me one first, sugarplum! What are you really doin' here in Deadman's Gulch?

Hughie (*after a big yawn*) Come to find Uncle Ossie...(*Yawn*) He had a ranch ...(*Yawn*) think Matt Vinyl stole it an' ... (*Yawn*) goin' to ... goin' to... (*another yawn and he falls asleep, snoring loudly*)

Lulabelle So that's why they're here! Wait till Matt hears about this!

She rushes out R

Hughie gives a loud snore and rolls off the bar out of sight

Mother (*off; calling*) Hughie? Hughie Hubbard, where are you?! Hughieeeee?!

She appears outside the swing doors and peers into the saloon. She is wearing another outrageous Wild West outfit

I hope he's not hangin' about in this den of iniquity! (*She calls*) Hughie?!

From behind the bar Hughie gives a loud snore

That's him! I'd recognize that fog horn anywhere!

She pushes open the doors and steps in. The doors hit her on the rebound. She creeps down c, *calling in a frightened whisper*

Hughie? I know you're in here somewhere! Come to your Mummy, at once! (*To the audience*) Hallo, folks! Have you seen him? Have you seen my Hughie?
Audience Behind the bar, *etc*!
Mother He's where?

After by-play, she goes up and looks behind the bar

(*Horrified*) Hughie Hubbard!!

Loud snore from Hughie

Look at the state of you! (*To the audience*) Just like 'is father! Pickled! (*She moves back to* c) Well, at least I've found him! I've been worried sick what he might say, he's so easily led, you see! Half a lemonade and he'd tell anyone anythin'! All about that nasty Matt Vinyl an'... 'Ere! He hasn't told anyone as he?!
Audience Yes!
Mother Oh, no! And do you think murky Matt is on 'is way to sort us out?!
Audience Yes!
Mother (*in a panic*) Oooh! Then I've got to get away an' warn the others! (*She rushes to the bar, bends over it and tries to rouse Hughie; ad lib*)

As she is doing so, Matt Vinyl enters from R and creeps up behind her

"Look out, he's behind you" routine with audience. Mother turns to look with Vinyl keeping behind her. Eventually, they come face to face. She yells and tries to make a run for it, but Vinyl grabs her

Unhand me, Vinyl! You underhanded undercoat, you!
Vinyl Ha! Ha! Ha! So! Thought you could outsmart Matt Vinyl, huh? Wull, I know everythin'!! Yur dimwit son spilled the beans! Sure! I took yur brother's ranch an' finished him off fer good! (*He pushes her back against the bar and pulls out his gun*)

Note : there must be enough room for the others to form a straight line across the stage during the following sequence

An' now I'm gonna do the same to you!

He slowly takes aim. Mother recoils

Tex rushes on from R and sticks his gun in Vinyl's back

Tex Reach fer it!

Vinyl's hands go up

Hank enters R and sticks his gun in Tex's back

Hank Reach fer it!

Tex's hands go up

Tumbleweed enters R and sticks his gun in Hank's back

Tumbleweed Reach fer it!

Hank's hands go up

Jake enters R and sticks his gun in Tumbleweed's back

Jake Reach fer it!

Tumbleweed's hands go up

Little Deer enters R *and sticks her finger in Jake's back*

Little Deer (*putting on a deep voice*) Reach fer it!

Jake's hands go up. Mother looks down the line

Mother That's the lot! We win!! Hurray!!
Tex (*stepping out of the line and keeping his gun trained on Vinyl*)
    Tumbleweed, git thar guns. An' don't you galoots try anythin'!

Tumbleweed collects guns from Vinyl and his boys. They lower their hands

Jake (*turning to see Little Deer*) That pesky Injun...(*he sees her finger
    sticking out*) ... with jist a finger!!
Tex (*to Vinyl*) Git over thar!

He gestures with his gun to DR. *They move*

*Polly and Dandy rush in through the swing doors. The crowd follow and
fill the back*

Polly What happened? Mum, are you all right?
Mother (*going to them*) Polly! Dandy! Oh, it was terrible! (*She points to
    Vinyl*) He was goin' to fill me full of holes! If Tex hadn't come in you
    could have used me as a colander! And it's all true! He did steal Ossie's
    ranch an' deaded 'im! He told me so himself!
Tex So, Vinyl! You admit it, huh?
Vinyl I ain't admittin' nothin'!! The old crow's gone plumb loco! She's
    makin' the whole thin' up!
Mother Oh, you great big fibber, you!
Vinyl Where's yur proof? Where's yur witnesses?!
Mother (*pointing to the audience*) Out there. (*To the audience*) He did
    say 'e did it, didn't 'e?!
Audience Yes!
Vinyl (*snarling at audience*) Oh, no, I din't! (*Routine with audience*)

Pah! You don't count! You ain't even suposed to be here!

Hughie groans loudly from behind the bar. All react

Polly What was that?
Mother Of course! Hughie! He must have heard everything!

She rushes to the bar and drags Hughie to c. He is feeling very unwell, to say the least

Here he is! My star witness!
Hughie (*groaning*) Oooh! My head!
Mother Never mind yer 'ead! Just get yer tongue workin' an' tell everyone what you heard old Mr Nasty say! Go on!
Hughie I... I... Ooo! I don't feel well! Ooo!!

He is about to collapse. Little Deer rushes over and holds him up

Vinyl (*sneering*) Ha! Some star witness!

He and his cronies roar with laughter. Tex confronts Vinyl and the laughter dies

Tex (*with icy calm*) Listen to me, Vinyl! I ain't gonna rest till I see justice carried out. I'm gonna make sure you stand trial fur what yuh done to Oswald Hubbard. I'll help rid this country of scum like you! You got Tex Laramie's word on it! (*To the others, moving to the swing doors*) Come on, folks. Time we was hittin' the trail.(*He ushers them out*)

Mother, Polly, Dandy, Hughie and Little Deer exit

(*To Vinyl*) You ain't seen the last of us.

He exits

Tumbleweed You sure ain't! No, siree! (*He spits off stage*)

Bell rings off stage

Tumbleweed exits

The crowd gather at the doors to watch the departure

Hank We gotta do somethin' fast, boss!

Jake Yeah! You heared what he said! He ain't gonna rest till he sees justice carried out! Oh, how I hate that word "justice"! Ugh!! (*He shivers*)

Vinyl Shut up! I'm thinkin'!

Hank Why don't we round up the boys, go after 'em, an' fill 'em full o' lead!

Jake Yeah! 'Specially that Injun gal! She got the drop on me with just her finger! I hate them sneaky Injuns.

Vinyl (*struck by the idea*) Injuns! Yeah! (*An evil plan formulating*) Yeah... that's it! (*He puts his arms around Hank and Jake, very pleased with himself*) Boys, we ain't gonna do nothin'!!

He laughs at their puzzlement

I'm gonna git someone else to take care of it fur us! Git my horse saddled up! I'm gonna pay a little visit on my old friend — Big Chief Thunder Cloud! (*He laughs, then yells*) Lulabelle! Git them dancers in here! We're losin' trade! What yuh think this place is — the (*local gag*) ?!!

He exits R *with Hank and Jake laughing*

The music strikes up. Lulabelle and her dancers run on and perform a short reprise of 10A

It ends with cheers and whistles from the crowd, as the Lights fade to Black-out

Scene 2

On the prairie. Tabs or the frontcloth used in Act 1, Scene 4. Sound of horses riding up and stopping off L

Tex and Polly enter from L, *followed by Little Deer and Hughie*

Polly Has your headache gone, Hughie?
Hughie No, but after all that ridin' it's moved! (*He rubs his sore bottom*)

The others laugh

Tex An hour in the saddle sure does yuh good!
Polly (*smiling*) I don't think Mum would agree with you!

Mother staggers on from L. She is bow-legged and very saddle-sore. Tumbleweed and Dandy follow her on

Mother (*to the audience, in agony*) Coo! Is there a tube of "Savlon" in the house?! Has anyone ever thought of givin' horses shock absorbers? Ooh! I'm numb from the knees up! All that up and down, up and down! I shall never be able to straighten out my chassis again!

The others laugh

(*In misery*) Oh, don't make fun of me! I'm just a dead-end kid!
Polly What are we going to do now, Tex? Vinyl is certain to come after us.
Tex Thar's an old abandoned cabin up in the hills. We kin use it fur a hideout. Once I git you settled in there I'll ride to Dodge City an' see the Marshal.
Polly Are you coming with us, Little Deer?
Little Deer (*sadly*) No, me no can come.
Hughie But you must! Vinyl knows you helped us. He'll be after you too.
Little Deer Me want um stay with Huu...eee! But no can disobey Father Big Chief. It law of tribe! (*Sadly*) Me go now.
Hughie But we might never see each other again!
Tex Sure you will! Listen Hughie! As soon as Vinyl's behind bars you kin see as much of Little Deer as you like. Time we was headin' fur the cabin! Let's hit the saddle!

He and Polly exit L

Mother (*groaning*) Oh, no! Not again! Just when the feelin' was comin' back! Can't we catch a bus?! I refuse to sit on that four-legged fiend again!

Tumbleweed (*leering*) I could always give yuh rub down first!

Mother (*calling*) Mr Horsey! Here I come!!

She runs out L followed by Tumbleweed and Dandy

Left alone Hughie and Little Deer sadly bid farewell. They kiss behind Hughie's hat

Hughie goes to exit L, stops to wave sadly, then exits

Little Deer goes to the exit and waves

Sound of horses riding away off L

Red Indian type music

Big Chief Thunder Cloud enters from R followed by his young son, Little Drizzle

Little Deer is unaware of them and continues waving off L. The Chief and Little Drizzle shade their eyes and look off L. This done, they move down c. The Chief faces front and folds his arms sternly. Little Drizzle copies his every movement. The music fades out

Chief (*to the audience; raising his hand in salute*) How!!

Audience How!!

Little Drizzle (*to the audience, trying to copy Chief's deep tone*) How!

Audience How!!

Startled, Little Deer turns and comes down to them

Little Deer Greetings, my father — Big Chief Thunder Cloud! Greetings, my brother — Little Drizzle!

Chief My daughter!

Little Drizzle My daughter!

Chief Why you wave?

Little Drizzle Why you wave?

Chief (*after a glare at Little Drizzle*) Me see five Pale Faces with dog!

Who Pale Face?!
Little Drizzle Who Pale Face?

Chief glares at Little Drizzle

Chief Answer! Who Pale Faces?
Little Deer They ... er ...they lost on prairie.
Chief Lost on prairie?
Little Drizzle Lost on prairie?
Chief (*roaring at him*) Put um sock in it! (*To the audience*) Him not papoose — him parrot! (*To Little Deer*) Why they lost?
Little Deer They looking for place called — (*local place*).
Chief Me go there once! It shut! (*He gives a deep laugh*) Ho! Ho! Ho!
Little Drizzle (*copying him*) Ho! Ho! Ho!
Chief (*roaring at him again*) Ahhhgr! Me no tell you again! When me get um you home, you be he who dances with sore bottom! Come! We go to camp! (*He turns to leave*)
Little Drizzle (*to the audience; raising his hand*) How!!
Chief (*to the audience; grabbing him by the ear*) Me show him how when me get um him home!

Two Indian braves enter from R *holding Matt Vinyl between them*

Little Deer reacts and keeps hidden behind the Chief

Vinyl Howdy, Thunder Cloud! I come in peace. D'you mind tellin' (*popular comedy duo*) to let me go. I've come fur a peaceful pow-wow.

The Chief signals to the braves and they release Vinyl

Chief Me know you! You Matt Vinyl! You heap big crook! You no friend to Indian!
Vinyl Wull, that's jist where you're wrong, Chief. I've come to give yuh a friendly warnin'! What do you think of (*a sinister pause*) the railroad?
Chief (*with disgust*) Pah! Railroad no good to Indian! Make Indian lose home. Make buffalo leave hunting grounds! Railroad no good! No run on time and heap big pollution!
Vinyl If I was to tell you there's plans to put a railroad slap bang in the middle of yur territory, what would yuh say?

Chief (*growling in anger*) Gerrrrr!!

Vinyl That's jist what I thought you'd say! An' if you got yur hands on the railroad people, what would yuh do to 'em?

Chief (*enraged*) Me scalp um!!

Vinyl That's jist what I thought you'd do! Wull, it's true, Chief! They do plan to put a railroad through here! The company have sent five agents to start organizing it. They're here right now!

Chief (*with growing suspicion*) Five Pale Faces! — with dog?!

Vinyl Yeah, they have gotta dog! Have you seen...

The Chief moves, revealing a terrified Little Deer

Chief Daughter! What you know about this?!

Vinyl Chief, I hate to tell yuh this but I seen yur daughter in town with them railroaders! I reckon she's in cahoots with 'em!

Chief (*roaring at her*) Ahhhgr!!

Little Deer (*frightened, but standing up to him*) It not true! He speak with fork tongue! They not from railroad! They —

Chief (*silencing her with a roar*) Ahhhgr!! You heap big disgrace to tribe! (*To Vinyl*) Where Pale Faces with dog now?

Vinyl I dunno. In hidin' someplace I guess! I bet she knows where!

Chief (*to Little Deer*) You tell!

Litttle Deer He lie! He make you do bad things! He —

Chief You tell! Honour of tribe at stake! You tell where find Pale Faces — now!

Little Deer (*duty bound*) They...they in old cabin in hills!

Chief You return to camp. Me deal um with you later!

Little Deer bursts into tears and runs out R

Vinyl What yuh gonna do now, Chief?

Chief Me go to camp! Get many braves! Put on designer war paint! Go to cabin! Kill railroad Pale Faces!

Vinyl (*to the audience, rubbing his hands*) Sounds mighty good to me! Ha! Ha! Ha!

Chief (*to Vinyl; raising his hand*) How!

Vinyl (*doing the same*) How!!

Little Drizzle How!!

Chief (*to the audience*) Him just like his Mother — must have um last word! (*To the others*) Come — we go on warpath!

Drums and Indian type music

*Led by the Chief, Little Drizzle and the braves do a war dance around
the stage and exit* R.. *Fade music*

Vinyl (*to the audience, with a gloating laugh*) Ha! Ha! Ha! That stupid
Injun! He'll git rid of Laramie and the others without me havin' to lift
a finger! An' if the law gits involved — wull, the Injuns'll git the blame!
Ha! Ha! You gotta hand it to me, I'm a real clever son of a gun, ain't I?
Oh, yes, I am! So long, sidewinders! See you at the scalpin'! Ha! Ha! Ha!

Laughing his evil laugh, he exits R, *amid boos and hisses*

Indian music as the Lights fade to Black-out

SCENE 3

*The cabin in the hills. A half set. The bare, dusty interior of a dilapidated
log cabin.* UC *is a practical door, with a view of the hills beyond. A practical
wooden beam is set* LC. *There are entrances* R *and* L. *Crude windows, a
crumbling stone fireplace, etc., can be painted on the scenery. The only
furniture is a rickety chair*

*Tex and Polly are discovered. The door is wide open and Polly is sweeping
out the dust with a broom. Tex is fixing a ragged, patched curtain to a
window*

Tex (*standing back and admiring his handiwork*) Thar! All the comforts
of the (*local posh hotel*).
Polly (*looking*) That's much better, Tex.
Tex Sorry it ain't more homely. It's the only place I could think of to use
fur a hideout.
Polly (*putting aside the broom*) I think it's perfect. I could feel really at
home here.
Tex (*moving to her, rather excited*) Yuh could?! I ... I got a hankerin' to
settle down myself. I'm gittin' tired o' this wanderin' life. Yep! I could
settle down mighty easy if... if ...

Polly (*as if she didn't know*) If what, Tex?
Tex (*taking her hands*) If I had someone like you to settle down with!

Song 13

After the duet, a loud crash and a yell is heard off L. *Tumbleweed blunders on with an upturned bucket stuck on his head. Mother follows him on, hitting the bucket with a broom. She now wears a very loud gingham dress with apron*

Mother (*hitting the bucket*) Take that! And that ! And that!

Tumbleweed staggers out of range to DR *and tries to get the bucket off*

Polly Mum! What on earth are you doing?
Mother Oh, Polly! I've 'ad it up to 'ere with that poor man's Box Car Willie! He was supposed to be 'elpin' me clean the floor in there! All I said was, I'm the best scrubber in the business, and he... well, I'll leave the rest to your imagination! He's beyond the pail, he really is! (*She puts the broom aside*)

Tex and Polly go to Tumbleweed's assistance and pull the bucket off his head

Tumbleweed Gol darn it! She coulda killed me!
Tex Why, did you nearly suffocate?
Tumbleweed Nope! Thar was some water left in the bucket! (*He shakes his head in disgust*) Yuck!!

A very downcast Hughie enters UC *followed by Dandy*

Mother (*to the audience*) Oh, look out! Here comes love's young dream!

Hughie gives an enormous sigh. Dandy does the same

(*Putting a comforting arm around him*) Come on, Hughie, luv! Try to snap out of it. You've got a face like (*local place*) on a wet weekend! You'll see your Little Deer again, don't worry so!

Hughie gives an even bigger sigh. Dandy does the same

Tex What he needs is somethin' to take his mind off things! Say, Hughie, come an' help us git some wood an' water fur the cabin.

He and Polly lead Hughie out UC. *Dandy trots out after them*

Mother, left alone with Tumbleweed, eyes him suspiciously. He winks at her

Mother Aren't you goin' with them?

Tumbleweed Nope! Reckon I'll stay here fur a piece.

Mother A piece of what, dare I ask?

Tumbleweed I gotta mighty big hunch.

Mother Well, don't pick it, an' it'll soon get better!

Tumbleweed I gotta hunch you could reely git to like me! I ain't bad lookin', am I?

Mother Compared to what?!

Tumbleweed An' I've bin around! Done all sorts! I kin put my hand to anythin'!!

Mother So I'd noticed!

Tumbleweed Yep! I've done it all! Prospectin'!! Ropin'! Ridin'!! Shootin'! And (*proudly*) I was the best cowpoke in three counties!

Mother Really?! I shan't ask for any details about that!

Tumbleweed (*with poetic passion*) Oh, come on! You kin be the little flower garden in my prairie wilderness!

Mother (*playing up to him*) How heavenly! And you can be the little compost heap at the bottom of it!! (*She pushes him away*)

Song 14

A comedy duet

It ends with Mother chasing Tumbleweed out UC

She shuts the door and leans against it, gasping for breath

(*To the audience*) Oh, it's my own fault for bein' so alluring! Ooh! That's tired me out! I shall 'ave to take a little nap! (*She flops down on the chair*) Now, listen kids! If old fungus face tries to creep up on me while I'm asleep, give me a shout. Will you do that? Oh, bless you! Right! Night, night! (*She goes to sleep, snoring loudly*)

The door slowly swings open. A huge Grizzly bear is framed in the doorway

The audience will be shouting, but Mother does not wake

The bear ambles in and starts inspecting the cabin. It sees Mother and moves behind her chair. She wakes with a start and jumps up

Eh!...What?! (*To the audience*) What is it? Is it old fungus face back again?

She comes forward with the bear keeping behind her

Is he 'ere now? Oh, he's behind me, is he? You know what I'm goin' to do? I'm just goin' to ignore 'im!

She sticks her nose in the air. The bear puts its arm around her and gives her a hug. She pulls free, and with an indignant toss of her head, folds her arms, and turns her back on the bear so that she faces the L entrance. The bear puts its arms around her waist and cuddles her

You won't get around me, you furry faced old fossil, you!

Tumbleweed enters L

He stops dead in his tracks and stares in dumb horror at the bear

Mother stares at him, then at the paws around her waist. She looks at the audience and screams

Tumbleweed screams and runs out L

Mother, yelling blue murder, pulls free and runs around the cabin being pursued by the bear

Dandy appears in the doorway

  He bounds in to the rescue, barking and growling

The bear stops chasing Mother and looks at the dog. Dandy stops barking and looks at the bear. They go forward to meet, rub noses, then shake paws

  They move up to the door, and Dandy courteously lets the bear exit in front of him. He gives Mother the "thumbs up" sign and trots out after the bear

  (*To the audience*) Well! Did you see that! I've heard of the "Dog and Duck", but that's ridiculous! Ooh! All this has been too much for me!!

Indian drums are heard in the distance. Mother reacts and puts her hand to her heart

  (*To the audience*) Can you 'ear that?! It's me poor old ticker goin' nineteen to the dozen!

Indian war whoops are heard outside. Mother freezes in terror

Hughie (*off; yelling*) Mum! Mum!!

  He enters UC. *He has several arrows sticking out of his hat*

  Mum! There's Indians everywhere!!
Mother And just look what they've done to your new 'at!
Hughie That's not all!

He turns round to show an arrow sticking out of the seat of his pants. Comic business as Mother pulls it out and throws it on the ground

  W...What are we goin' to do, Mum?!
Mother Shut the door!

They do so. Hughie grabs the chair and rams it under the door handle. The Indian war whoops fade out. Hughie and Mother peer out through the cracks in the door with their backs to the room

They can't get at us now, Hughie!
Hughie No, we're safe now, Mum!

Two Indian braves creep on from R. They wear war paint and brandish fearsome looking tomahawks

The audience will be shouting but Mother and Hughie take no notice. They wait until the braves are right behind them, then do a slow turn to face front

Mother (*to Hughie; indicating the audience*) What's that lot shoutin' about?

They move down stage with the Indians keeping behind them

(*To the audience*) What's the matter? Indians? No, they can't get in!
Hughie (*to the audience*) No, we've shut the door!

"Behind you!" routine with the audience. Finally, they come face to face with the braves, who grab them and drag them to RC

Mother (*yelling*) Help! I've been grabbed by the Chippewas!!

The door bursts open and Chief Thunder Cloud strides in, followed by Little Drizzle and several armed braves

The Chief peers closely at Mother

Didn't your Mummy tell you it was rude to stare?! (*She looks at his head-dress. To the audience*) So that's what 'appened to our Christmas turkey!
Chief (*roaring at her*) Ahhhgrrr!!

She recoils

Little Drizzle (*roaring at her*) Ahhhgrr!!
Mother (*to the audience*) Now he's more my size! (*She roars at Little Drizzle*) Ahhhgrr!

Little Drizzle hides behind the Chief

Chief We take um you to camp!
Mother Oh, are we goin' to 'ave a jamboree?

The Chief signals to braves and they haul Mother and Hughie to the door

They are dragged out and off to R. *The Chief, Little Drizzle and the other braves follow*

The drum beats fade out

A slight pause, and Matt Vinyl appears in the doorway from off L. *He watches the departure, then enters the cabin. Hank and Jake follow him in*

Hank It sure looks like yur plan worked, boss!
Vinyl Yeah. But the redskins only got two of 'em! There's still Tex Laramie, the gal and the old-timer to take keer of!
Polly (*off; calling*) Mum! Where are you??!
Tex (*off; calling*) Hughie?!
Vinyl That's them! Let's hide!

They rush out R

Tex, Polly and Tumbleweed run in through the doorway UC

Polly (*calling*) Mum! Hughie! Where are you?!
Tumbleweed (*coming down and picking up the arrow*) Hey, Tex! Lookee here!
Tex (*examining it*) This is one of Thunder Cloud's arrows! His tribe's usually peaceful! What in tarnation's goin' on here?!

Vinyl and his boys creep on from R *with their guns drawn. Hank carries a coil of rope. Vinyl has a tin can marked "Kerosene"*

Polly Do you think the Indians have got Mum and Hughie?
Tex It sure looks that way!
Vinyl Reach for it!

The others spin round

I said reach for it!

Tex and the others put their hands up

Git over against that beam!

They do so

Jake, git their guns!

Jake takes their guns, sticks them in his belt and rejoins Vinyl

I told Thunder Cloud you was here to build a railroad across his lands.
He's mighty riled up about it! He's took the old woman an' her son to
his camp. He was supposed to deal with you too, but I'm gonna do that
— personally! Hank, tie 'em up!

*Hank ties Tex and others to the beam, then rejoins his cronies. Vinyl puts
his gun away, and holds up the tin of kerosene. He laughs devilishly as the
others react with horror. He unscrews the top*

Never let it be said that Matt Vinyl don't give strangers a warm
welcome!

*He and his side-kicks guffaw. The others struggle in vain to get free. Vinyl
sprinkles the kerosene about. He throws the empty tin aside and takes out
a box of matches. Gloating, he rattles it at the others. They freeze in terror*

*Slowly, as Vinyl extracts a match, the Grizzly bear appears in the
doorway behind them*

The bear gives a mighty roar. They spin around and shriek at what they see. Vinyl drops the matches and all three run around being chased by the bear

   Dandy bounds in and joins the chase

   Finally, Vinyl and his boys manage to escape through the door

Comic business as Dandy and the bear give each other "some skin". Dandy bites the rope, setting the others free

Polly (*hugging him*) Oh, Dandy, you saved us! You saved our lives!
Dandy (*indicating the bear*) Woof! Woof!
Polly (*rather unsure*) Oh, yes... er... and your friend. (*She moves cautiously to the bear*) T... Thank you... er... Mr Bear.

Rather surprisingly, the bear gives her an elegant bow. The others react. Dandy shakes paws with the bear

   It goes to the door, turns and waves at everyone (including the audience) then ambles out

We've got to save Mum and Hughie from the Indians!
Tumbleweed With no shootin' irons?!
Tex Thar's only one thing fur it! I'll ride to Fort Mason! This is a job for the cavalry!
Polly We'll come with you!
Tumbleweed Sure!
Dandy Woof!!
Tex Nope! I'll travel better alone. You stay right here, I'd best be movin'!! So long!

   He runs out back c

Polly, Tumbleweed and Dandy pace up and down the cabin floor

Polly Oh, I feel so helpless!
Dandy (*agreeing*) Woof!
Polly Poor Mum and Hughie! There must be something we can do to help!

Tumbleweed I know where the Injun's camp is — (*not so sure*) least ways, I reckon I could follow their trail.
Dandy (*pointing to himself*) Woof! Woof! (*He sniffs around like a bloodhound*)
Polly So could Dandy! He's got the best nose in the business!
Tumbleweed Then what in tarnation are we waitin' fer?! Let's vamoose out of here!

They run out UC

Indian music that continues into the next scene. The Lights fade to Black-out

SCENE 4

On the prairie. Tabs or the frontcloth used in Act 2, Scene 2

Chief Thunder Cloud enters from L, *followed by Little Drizzle and two braves, dragging an exhausted Mother and Hughie. She stops, refusing to go any further. The music fades out*

Mother Oy! Big Chief Thunder Bucket or whatever your name is! I refuse to go another step! Me poor old feet are worn down to the knee caps! I demand a rest stop! I know my rights as an English woman and a fully paid up member of the (*local gag*)!
Chief You got no rights! You going to die!
Mother (*gulping; in a small voice*) I... I'd still like a little rest.
Chief You get heap big rest when me scalp um you! (*Deep laugh*) Ho! Ho! Ho!
Little Drizzle Ho! Ho! Ho!
Hughie Ho! Ho! Ho!
Mother Ho! Ho! Ho! (*Aside to Hughie*) I don't know what we're laughin' at! He's goin to scalp um us — what ever that means!
Hughie It means he's goin' to cut our hair off——
Mother Oo, nice! I fancy a new look!
Hughie — with a big knife!
Mother Oh, like at (*local hairdressers*) you mean? That's a bit daft, isn't it ? Givin' us a hair cut then killin' us!

Hughie It's the hair cut that kills us! They cut off the hair with the scalps attached!

Mother puzzles this out, then the awful truth dawns on her. She gulps and goes weak at the knees

Mother (*to Chief*) Is...is that true?
Chief True!
Little Drizzle True!

Comic business as Mother collapses back into Hughie's arms

Chief (*very proudly*) Me have many scalps. Me partner in "Wild West Wig Company"!
Hughie Where do you keep 'em all, in your — Wigwam?
Mother He keepee toupee in teepee!

They both laugh, then remember their situation and the laughter turns into a wail

Chief You no laugh when me scalp um you!
Mother (*to the audience; resigned*) Oh, well! Hair today and gone tomorrow!
Chief Come! We go now!
Little Drizzle Come! We go now!

The Chief signals to the braves and they grab hold of Mother and Hughie

Mother (*to a brave*) Careful, Minnehaha! You pinch me again and I'll catch you unawares in your Delawares!
Hughie Steady, Mum! Keep your hair on!
Mother (*wailing*) Ooo! Don't remind me!

They are dragged off to R. *Chief and Little Drizzle follow*

A slight pause. Dandy enters L, *sniffing out the trail. He is closely followed by Tumbleweed who is on his hands and knees, looking for tracks*

Polly enters behind him

At c Dandy stops dead, causing a bit of a pile up! They sort themselves out and Dandy picks up the scent again. He moves all around the stage, sniffing. Tumbleweed and Polly follow him in single file with heads bent to the ground

Unseen by them, the two braves enter from R *and join on the end of the line*

The audience will be shouting but no-one takes any notice. The braves follow the others around once, then stand still on R. *Eventually, Dandy's nose comes in contact with the brave's feet. He gives them a puzzled sniff, then looks up. So do Tumbleweed and Polly. Dandy howls and the other two yell. The braves grab Tumbleweed and Polly*

Dandy runs off R

The braves start to drag the others towards R *exit, as Matt Vinyl enters from* L

Vinyl (*raising his hand to braves*) How!! (*He moves* C *with a sneering laugh*) Ha! Ha! So! It looks as if Thunder Cloud will soon have a full set!
Polly Your plan isn't going to work, Vinyl! Tex has gone to Fort Mason to get help!

Vinyl just laughs and signals off L

Hank and Jake enter, dragging Tex between them

Tex!
Tex I'm sorry, honey! I didn't get through. These sidewinders bushwacked me!
Vinyl Ha! Ha! Ha! Come on! Don't let's keep the Chief waitin'! I bet he's got his scalpin' knife all nice an' sharp!

He and his cronies laugh

The braves drag Polly and Tumbleweed out R

Hank and Jake follow with Tex

Vinyl turns to the audience

An' when he's done with them, I'll git him to scalp some of you! — with
a blunt knife! Ha! Ha! An' I'll tell him not to stop at jist cuttin' off yer
hair! Ha! Ha! Ha!

He exits R *amid boos and hisses*

Little Deer creeps on from L, *followed by Dandy*

Little Deer (*to the audience, in great distress*) What me going to do?!
  Must save Hughie and others! But not know how! You know how,
  Dandy?
Dandy (*nodding eagerly*) Woof! Woof!
Little Deer You tell Little Deer how!

Dandy points to her

Me?

He nods and demonstrates running

Run?

He nods

Me run where?

He makes a big square shape in the air

Me run to house?

He shakes his head and makes a much bigger square

Me run to block of flats?

He shakes his head and gallops up and down as if riding a horse

Me run to Goodwood?

He shakes his head and mimes drawing a sword and waving it madly about

Me run to Wimbledon?

He shakes his head. He is now getting frustrated. He mimes blowing a bugle

Me run to jazz concert?

He shakes his head, and wildly gallops up and down while blowing the bugle and waving the sword

Me run to (*local event*) ?

Frustrated and exhausted Dandy collapses C *and covering his head with his paws, gives a despairing whine. Little Deer turns to the audience*

Me no understand what he mean! Where he want me to run?
Audience To the fort!

Dandy raises his paw and gives the audience the "thumbs up" sign

Little Deer (*to the audience*) Ah! Me run to fort! Get help! Me go!

She runs to exit L *but Matt Vinyl appears there*

Little Deer backs away as he advances on her

She turns to run off R *but Hank and Jake enter and grab her*

Dandy observes this, but remains where he is pretending to be just a simple dog

Vinyl Let's take her to the Chief! I figger he'll wanta punish his naughty little girl!

Hank (*pointing to Dandy*) What about the dawg, boss?

Acting silly, Dandy rolls over on his back and kicks his legs in the air

Vinyl Leave him! Look! He's jist a crazy, dumb mutt!

They exit R, with Little Deer

As soon as they are out of sight, Dandy leaps up and bounds out L

Indian music that continues into the next scene. The Lights fade to Blackout

SCENE 5

The Red Indian camp. Full set. UC is a fearsome, many-headed totem pole. Large and prominent on L is the chief's teepee. A much smaller teepee is on R. The side wings depict more teepees, rocks and trees. The backcloth shows the rest of the camp with mountains in the distance

Drums and Indian type music. Slowly, the lighting comes up to reveal the Indians, frozen in a tableau depicting everyday life in an Indian village. Pause for effect, then the music changes and the Indians come to life and go into a song

Song 15

After the song, Chief Thunder Cloud emerges from his teepee, followed by Little Drizzle. The Indians solemnly pay homage

Suddenly, the frightening figure of the Medicine Man leaps on from DR. He wears a fierce mask and a head-dress with huge horns, a long bear's tooth necklace and carries a feathered rattle. He does a strange little dance on the spot, while emitting high-pitched yelps and shaking the rattle

When Medicine Man has finished:

Chief (*to the audience*) Him heap big Medicine Man! We call —

The man squirms and gives a couple of yelps

—he who dances with tight Y-fronts!

Medicine Man goes to Chief and talks in wild gibberish

(*To the audience*) He asks, when do we kill Pale Faces?
Medicine Man (*nodding eagerly*) Ug! Ug!
Chief (*to Medicine Man*) We kill Pale Faces when (*in grand manner with lots of hand movements*) mighty sun sink low in West, and golden eagle fly to nest. When shadows fall on old pine tree and tired Indian comes home for tea! (*To Medicine Man, very matter of fact*) Five o'clock.

Very excited, the Medicine Man does a leap in the air and runs out down R yelping and shaking his rattle

(*To the audience*) Himvery keen!

Matt Vinyl enters down L followed by Hank and Jake, dragging Little Deer

Vinyl (*raising his hand to Chief*) How!!
Chief How!! What you do with wayward daughter?
Vinyl We caught her tryin' to fetch help fur the railroad Pale Faces.

The Chief and all the Indians gasp in horror

Chief (*to Little Deer*) This true?
Little Deer Yes ...

The Indians gasp again

But they not bad Pale Faces! He speak with fork tongue! Father must listen to Little Deer!
Chief (*silencing her with an angry growl*) Ahhgrr! (*He turns to front and folds his arms*) Me make heap big decision! Honour of tribe at stake!(*To Little Deer*) You like so much — you die with them!

General sensation. Chief signals to a brave, who takes Little Deer DL *and ties her hands behind her back*

Vinyl (*to Chief, during this*) I think you're doin' the right thing, Chief. You gotta set an example.

Chief (*to Indians*) Bring out! Is time for scalping ceremony!

Solemn drum beat starts, under the dialogue

Two braves go into the small teepee on R

Vinyl Say, Chief, it'd be a great honour fur me an' my boys to stay an' watch this!

Chief (*with a wave of his hands*) Be um guest! (*He clears to* L)

Sneering, Vinyl and his cronies move DR

The first brave comes out of the teepee R *followed by Tex, Polly, Hughie, Tumbleweed, Mother and second brave*

They all have their hands (supposedly) tied behind their backs. The braves push them into a line across C. *The Chief signals to the brave and he puts Little Deer in to the line up next to Hughie*

(*In a mighty voice*) Let Ceremonial Dance begin! (*He claps his hands and clears to* L)

The drum beats increase. The lighting changes to red, flickering fire effect

With wild yelps, the scantily clad dancers run on

The music starts

Dance 16

This should be a spectactular dance number performed by either a solo dancer (male or female) or a troupe, according to availability and space

A climactic ending, and the dancers run off, yelping wildly. Cut music

The lighting returns to normal. The solemn drum beat continues under dialogue

Mother (*to the audience*) That beats the (*local dancing club*)! (*Or if male dancers are used*) Coo! Buy me one of those, Daddy!
Indians (*hissing loudly at her*) Shhh!!
Mother (*reacting*) Charming!

The Medicine Man's rattle is heard off L

Mother 'Ello! Sounds like someone's got big end trouble!

The Medicine Man enters DL doing a strange shuffling dance and shaking his rattle

(*To the audience*) Oh, look! I think it's (*pop-singer*)!

Medicine Man gives a couple of yelps

It is!

He shuffles along the line, shaking his rattle at each one. Finally, he gets to Mother

Hey (*pop-singer*) give that back to baby at once!

She reacts at his head-dress

'Ere! So you're the one who swiped the 'andle bars off my bike!

Medicine Man shuffles to C, raises his arms and shakes the rattle wildly. He gives a loud yelp, then drops to his knees and remains silent, with bowed head

(*To the audience, sighing*) Ahh! His Duracell's run out!
Chief (*in a mighty voice*) Bring Ceremonial Scalping Knife! (*He claps his hands*)

The drum beats increase

A brave, or one of the dancers, enters DL *holding a huge, gleaming knife*

All react and Mother lets out a wail. The Medicine Man rises and takes the knife. He holds it aloft. The drum beats stop. A deadly hush falls. He goes up and looks along the line. The prisoners are frozen with fear. He picks on Mother and points at her with the knife. She yells as a brave forces her to her knees. Medicine Man advances on her with knife at the ready. Suddenly a bugle is heard sounding the charge off stage. Shots are heard

All the Indians, except the Chief and Little Drizzle, panic and run off UC

At the same time, Dandy bounds on from DL. *He leaps at the Medicine Man and knocks him to the ground, where he remains unconscious*

Major Day, of the US Cavalry, runs on from DL *followed by two armed soldiers*

Vinyl and his boys are about to make a run for it DR *but the sudden appearance of a third soldier there stops them*

Major (*to soldiers*) Men! Untie those civilians!

The two soldiers go up and release the prisoners. Tex embraces Polly. Hughie embraces Little Deer. Tumbleweed embraces Mother

(*Saluting to them*) Major Day, US Cavalry! That's a mighty smart dog you've got there. He came to the fort an' made us follow him right back here!

Mother and the others make a great fuss of Dandy. He puts his foot on the Medicine Man and strikes a pose

(*Confronting the Chief*) Thunder Cloud, what's all this about? Your tribe has always bin peaceful.
Chief Me only defend property! They come build railroad on Indian land!
Tex There ain't gonna be no railroad! (*He points to Vinyl*) That dirty

Tex There ain't gonna be no railroad! (*He points to Vinyl*) That dirty skunk's responsible fur all this! Matt Vinyl. He told the Chief we was frum the Railroad Company! He wanted the Injuns to do his dirty work! He wanted us out of the way!

Mother Yes! Because we know all about him nobblin' my brother Ossie an' stealin his ranch!

Vinyl Ha! This is hogwash! They're makin' the whole thin' up!

Mother (*to Major*) Don't just stand there, Colonel Custard! Arrest that crook!

Major (*unsure*) Wull... without some kind of proof ...

Vinyl Ha! They ain't got no proof!

The Medicine Man starts groaning loudly. The others clear to reveal him trying to sit up

Medicine Man (*dazed*) Oh... My head! W...Where am I....? W...What happened?...Oo!

All react, not least Mother. She goes to him

Mother That voice! It...it can't be... (*She pulls off his mask/headdress*) It is! It's my brother Ossie!!

General sensation! Oswald is helped to his feet. He is very confused. Vinyl tries to exit, but the soldier blocks his way

Oswald (*peering at Mother*) Sissy? ...My sister? ... Is it really you?

Mother Yes, it is! Your own little sister! Oh, Ossie! (*She hugs him very tightly to her chest*)

Oswald Yes... Yes, I recognize you now. (*He looks around and sees Vinyl*) I... I think I know you too! You... (*He puts his hand to his head*) Oh, I...I'm so confused!

Tex His name's Matt Vinyl! He had somethin' to do with yur ranch!

Oswald M... my ranch? (*He gradually remembers*) Yes... Yes!! It's coming back to me now! It was late one night. Matt Vinyl and his boys came to see me. He said he was going to take over my ranch! I tried to fight, but... they took me out on to the prairie, and... and knocked me on the head!

Tex Well, Major, is that proof enough?

Others Yipee! Hurray, *etc.*
Major Men! Get their guns!

The soldiers disarm the cowed villains

I'm takin' you straight to Dodge City an' handin' you over to the Marshal!
Hughie Why don't you hand him over to them? (*He points to the audience. To them*) What would you like to do to him, kids?

By-play with the audience

Then, led by the Major, Vinyl and his boys are escorted out down L. They shake their fists and snarl at the others as they go

Everyone moves forward

The Indians return and fill the back

Polly Uncle Ossie, I still don't understand how you became an Indian Medicine Man.
Oswald I wish I knew myself!
Chief Thunder Cloud explain! Hunting party find you on prairie! You left for dead! You not know own name! Suffer from magnesia! Old Medicine Man take care of you! He take shine to you and teach you tricks of trade! When old Medicine Man retire to (*local watering place*) I make you new Medicine Man!
Mother (*to the audience*) That's neat, isn't it? (*Double take*) Well, what do you expect! It's only a flippin' fairy story!
Chief (*to Mother*) Thunder Cloud heap big sorry. Hope you accept apologies for unruly behaviour!
Mother Well, it was a close shave! But, I'll forgive you under the circumferences.
Tex (*to Mother*) Ma'am, I'd like to ask yer permission to marry Miss Polly an' settle down here.
Mother (*taken aback*) Er...well, only if Polly wants to ...

Polly embraces Tex

(*To the audience*) She wants to!

Hughie (*to Chief; nervously*) Er... Sir! Your Chieffulness, I'd like to ask your permission to marry Dittle Leer, I... I mean, Little Deer.

Chief Me give um consent! Me make you member of tribe! Ho! Ho! Ho!

He slaps Hughie on the back, knocking him into Little Deer's arms. General rejoicing, but Mother is downcast. Polly, Hughie and Dandy move to her, making a separate family group

Polly What's the matter, Mum?

Mother (*getting weepy*) Oh, dear! All my little chicks leavin' the nest! What am I goin' to do? (*Big sigh*) I'll have to go back home, I suppose.

Hughie Stay with us! There's only the unpaid rent to go back to!

Polly Yes. Besides, how will you get back? The Fairy only granted one wish, and that's been fulfilled! You've found Uncle Ossie.

Mother That's true! Oh, I don't know what to do! What do you think, Dandy? Shall I stay?

Dandy (*nodding vigorously*) Woof! Woof!

Mother That settles it! (*She moves* c *to everyone*) Pard'ners! I'm a stayin' put!

All Hurray! Yipee!! *etc.*

Oswald You can help me start my ranch up again. You were always fond of cows.

Mother Yes! Some of my best friends are old cows!

Tumbleweed (*moving to her*) An' I'll be there to help yuh out — with the brandin' iron! (*He jabs her in the bottom*)

She yells. Everyone roars with laughter

Chief Only one thing left to say! (*He raises his hand to Mother*) How!

Mother (*acting coy*) Oh, Chiefee! Me know how! You say when!

Everyone turns to the audience and raises their hands in salute

All (*to the audience*) How!

The music starts and everyone goes into a joyful song and dance

Song 17

After the song, a frontcloth is lowered or the tabs close

SCENE 6

The last round-up. Hughie and Dandy run on

Hughie (*to the audience, waving*) Howdy, kids!

They shout back

Did you hear anything, Dandy?
Dandy (*shaking his head*) Woof!
Hughie Neither did I! (*To the audience*) Come on, you can do better than
that! I want a really loud "Howdy, Hughie". Take the roof off! (*He
shouts to them*) Howdy, kids!

They shout back

And again, even louder! Howdy, kids!

They roar back

Mother runs on, carrying a US mail bag

Mother Oy! Wyatt Twerp! Deputy Dawg! The stage has just come into
town an' delivered this ! (*She holds up the bag*)
Hughie Who's it from, Mum?
Mother The Milky Bar Kid! An' he says "The Milky Bars are on me!"

*From the bag she throws out chocolate bars to the audience. After
business*

And there's something else! Big Chief Thunder Cloud wants to make
you all members of his tribe!
Hughie That's great!
Mother But, there's something they've all got to do first!

*The song sheet is lowered, or can be brought on by Little Drizzle and the
Grizzly bear. Comic business as Mother, Hughie, and Dandy get the
audience to sing along. A song with a Western flavour*

After the song sheet is removed, Mother, Hughie and Dandy wave goodbye to the audience and run out, as the Lights fade to Black-out

SCENE 7

The finale. A special settting or the Indian camp scene can be used with modifications

Music

All enter singing for Finale walkdown. The last to enter is Mother Hubbard, wearing an outrageous Indian Squaw costume

Tex	So long, pard'ners. It's the end of the trail.
Polly	We hope you have enjoyed this tale.
Hughie	To the Indian life I must kow tow!
Little Deer	In my wigwam me show you how!
Vinyl	I'll git yuh all, when I'm back in the saddle!
Chief	You up um creek without um paddle!
Tumbleweed(*to Mother*)	That outfit sure gives me sensations!
Mother (*warding him off*)	Keep yer' 'ands off my reservations!
Little Drizzle	Dandy no can speak pow-wow, but he is really nice.
Dandy	Bow-wow!
Fairy	The Hubbard family have been truly blessed, Finding this home in the Old Wild West, I'm glad they found me in their cupboard.
All	Good-night and God bless —from Old Mother Hubbard!

Final Song 19

CURTAIN

FURNITURE AND PROPERTY LIST

ACT I

SCENE 1

On stage :   Two baskets. *In them* : bundles of firewood (**Mother and Polly**)
               Large sign (**Children**)

Personal :   **Mother**: large, gaudy, handkerchief
               First Bailiff: eviction order

SCENE 2

Off stage: Two baskets. *In them* : bundles of firewood (**Polly** and **Hughie**)
               Bulging shopping bag. *In it*: sausages, toilet roll, packets of sweets (**First Woman**)

SCENE 3

Off stage :   Eviction order (**First Bailiff**)

Personal :   **Good Fairy**: magic wand

SCENE 4

Off stage :   Guitar (**Chorus**)
               Mouth organ (**Chorus**)

Personal :   **Tex** : gun (worn throughout)
               Tumbleweed : pouch of chewing tabacco, bottle

SCENE 5

Off stage :   Collecting tin. *In it* : coins (**Vinyl**)
               Lasso (**Hughie**)
               Trick lasso (**Dandy**)

Personal :   **Vinyl**: gun in a holster
                 Hank: gun in a holster
                 Jake: gun in a holster

ACT II

SCENE 1

On stage :   Bottles, glasses on bar
                 Tables and chairs
                 One large glass

SCENE 2

On stage :   Nil

SCENE 3

On stage :   Rickety, old chair
                 Broom

Off stage :   Broom (**Mother**)
                 Bucket (**Tumbleweed**)
                 Duplicate hat with arrows (**Hughie**)
                 Trick arrow in seat of trousers (**Hughie**)
                 Tomahawks (**Indian Braves**)
                 Coil of rope (**Hank**)
                 Can marked "Kerosene" (**Vinyl**)

Personal :   **Vinyl**: box of matches

SCENE 4

On stage :   Nil

Off stage :   Tomahawks (**Braves**)

SCENE 5

On stage: Many-headed totem pole
                 Rope (**Brave**)

Huge, gleaming knife (**Brave**)

Off stage :   Nil

Personal :   **Medicine Man**: fierce mask, head-dress, long bear's
tooth necklace, feathered rattle

SCENE 6

On stage :   Nil

Off stage :   US mail bag. *In it* : chocolate bars (**Mother**)

SCENE 7

On stage :   Nil

LIGHTING PLOT

Property fittings required: nil
Various interior and exterior settings

ACT I, SCENE 1

To open : Full general lighting

Cue 1	After reprise of Song 3 *Fade to black-out*	(Page 11)

ACT I, SCENE 2

To open : Exterior lighting

Cue 2	**Hughie:** "No, he's quite tame! Come on!" *House lights go up*	(Page 12)
Cue 3	Children return to their seats *House lights go down*	(Page 13)
Cue 4	Magical music *Lighting changes slightly*	(Page 14)
Cue 5	**Dandy** scampers out after the others *Lights fade to black-out*	(Page 15)

ACT I, SCENE 3

To open : Interior lighting

Cue 6	**Mother** opens the cupboard door wide *Eerie light on Fairy*	(Page 19)

Cue 7   A blinding flash   (Page 20)
            Black-out

Cue 8   **Mother** : "They've cut off me juice!! "   (Page 20)
            Full general lighting

Cue 9   **Fairy** waves her wand. Magical music   (Page 22)
            Stage grows dark. Spotlights come up on the group and
                Fairy

Cue 10   A blinding flash   (Page 22)
            Complete black-out

ACT I, Scene 4

To open: Bright exterior lighting

Cue 11   Sound of shattering glass   (Page 31)
            Black-out

ACT I, Scene 5

To open: Full general lighting

Cue 12   **Vinyl** moves to **Hank** and **Jake** DL   (Page 36)
            Stage grows dark. Green spotlight on Vinyl and his two
                cronies

Cue 13   **Vinyl** and his two cronies slap their holsters   (Page 37)
            The lighting returns to normal

ACT II, Scene 1

To open: Full general lighting. Saloon

Cue 14   Short reprise of 10A ends   (Page 51)
            Lights fade to black-out

ACT II, Scene 2

To open: Exterior lighting

Cue 15   Indian music   (Page 56)
          Lights fade to black-out

ACT II, Scene 3

To open: Interior lighting

Cue 16   **Polly, Tumbleweed** and **Dandy** run out uc   (Page 65)
          Lights fade to black-out

ACT II, Scene 4

To open: Exterior lighting

Cue 17   **Dandy** bounds out L. Indian Music   (Page 70)
          Lights fade to black-out

ACT II, Scene 5

To open: Exterior lighting

Cue 18   Drum beats increase   (Page 72)
          Lighting changes to red, flickering fire effect

Cue 19   The dancers run off, yelping wildly   (Page 73)
          Lighting returns to normal

ACT II, Scene 6

To open: Full general lighting

Cue 20   **Mother, Hughie and Dandy** run out   (Page 79)
          Lights fade to black-out

EFFECTS PLOT

Cue 1   The **Children** exit quickly into the cottage   (Page 8)
Music

Cue 2   The **Bailiffs** fall over   (Page 8)
Cut music

Cue 3   Polly: ".. be our last meal in the dear old cottage." (Page 14)
Magical music

Cue 4   The **Fairy** enters   (Page 14)
Fade magical music

Cue 5   Polly : " ... something to soak your feet!"   (Page 15)
Music

Cue 6   As Scene 2 finishes   (Page 15)
Fade music

Cue 7   **Mother** yells and tries to make a get-away   (Page 18)
"Hurry" music

Cue 8   The **Fairy** waves her wand   (Page 22)
Magical music plays

Cue 9   The **Fairy** points her wand at the group   (Page 22)
A blinding flash

Cue 10   The **Fairy** and **Dandy** exit   (Page 22)
Magical music becomes louder and more dramatic.
Strange, weird noises are heard

Cue 11   When ready   (Page 22)
Flash. Music and sounds fade out

Cue 12	**Tumbleweed** spits off stage L *A bell rings off stage* L	(Page 27)
Cue 13	**Tumbleweed** spits *Bell rings off stage* R	(Page 29)
Cue 14	**Tumbleweed** spits *Sound of shattering glass*	(Page 30)

ACT II

Cue 15	The dancers parade off L *Two loud shots are heard off* R	(Page 40)
Cue 16	**Tumbleweed** spits off stage *Bell rings off stage*	(Page 50)
Cue 17	To open Scene 2 *Sound of horses riding up and stopping off* L	(Page 51)
Cue 18	**Little Deer** goes to the exit and waves *Sound of horses riding away off* L. *Red Indian type music*	(Page 53)
Cue 19	The **Chief** faces front and folds his arms *Music fades*	(Page 53)
Cue 20	**Chief**: "Come we go on war path!" *Drums and Indian-type music*	(Page 56)
Cue 21	**Indians** exit R *Fade music*	(Page 56)
Cue 22	**Vinyl** exits R *Indian music*	(Page 56)
Cue 23	After **Song 13** *Loud crash is heard off* L	(Page 57)

Cue 24   **Mother:** " ... been too much for me!"   (Page 60)
            Indian drums are heard in the distance

Cue 25   The **Chief, Little Drizzle** exit   (Page 62)
            The drum beats fade out

Cue 26   **Polly, Tumbleweed** and **Dandy** run out UC   (Page 65)
            Indian music

Cue 27   **Mother** stops, refusing to go any further   (Page 65)
            Music fades out

Cue 28   **Dandy** leaps up and bounds out L   (Page 70)
            Indian music

Cue 29   As Scene 5 opens   (Page 70)
            Drums and Indian music

Cue 30   Lighting comes up to reveal **Indians**   (Page 70)
            Cut music

Cue 31   **Chief:** "Is time for scalping ceremony!"   (Page 72)
            Solemn drum beat starts

Cue 32   **Chief** claps his hands and clears to L   (Page 72)
            The drum beats increase

Cue 33   With wild yelps, the scantily clad dancers run on (Page 72)
            Music starts

Cue 34   When ready   (Page 73)
            Cut music

Cue 35   Lighting returns to normal   (Page 73)
            The solemn drum beat continues under the dialogue

Cue 36   **Chief** claps his hands   (Page 73)
            The drum beats increase